REAL ESTATE ACCOUNTING AND REPORTING

Real Estate Accounting and Reporting

A GUIDE FOR DEVELOPERS, INVESTORS AND LENDERS

JAMES J. KLINK

Partner, Price Waterhouse & Co.

A RONALD PRESS PUBLICATION

JOHN WILEY & SONS, New York · Chichester · Brisbane · Toronto

Library of Congress Cataloging in Publication Data:

Klink, James J   1931-
  Real estate accounting and reporting.

  "A Ronald Press publication."
  Includes index.
  1. Real estate business—Accounting. I. Title.

HF5686.R3K57   657′.833   80-11274
ISBN 0-471-06041-0

Printed in the United States of America

10 9 8 7 6 5 4

Preface

This book provides a compendium of accounting and financial reporting guidance in the unique environment of real estate, the nation's third largest industry. The interacting forces in this complex industry include investors, builders, developers, contractors, managers, mortgage lenders, governmental agencies, and professional accountants.

It is the author's purpose to help management of real estate entities fully understand the appropriate accounting for real estate transactions. It is also to provide those who utilize financial statements of real estate entities with a basis for making informed decisions. For the investor and mortgage lender—whether a bank, savings and loan association, real estate trust, or insurance company—the book provides tools for gaining significant insights into the entity's financial condition. It provides an understanding of accounting considerations and assistance for analytical analysis. For the professional accountant, it offers a wide range of practical guidance.

The book discusses current real estate accounting literature and provides illustrative examples and appropriate interpretive comment. Based upon the author's extensive real estate experience, there is a straightforward review of accounting for real estate acquisition, development, and construction costs, sales of real estate, and investments in real estate ventures. There are also comprehensive discussions on financial reporting and analysis. The accounting review covers the specialized problems of retail land developers, sales of condominiums, and investments in operations of real estate ventures. In addition, the book examines the problems of historical cost financial statements and the directions in which future financial reporting may evolve.

Grateful acknowledgment and sincere thanks are due to many people for their assistance in preparing the book, particularly Steven L. Brinser, James M. Degnan, Edward C. Harris, James O. Stepp, William Stoddart, and Edward V. Williams. However, the responsibility for the opinions and conclusions expressed in these pages is solely the author's.

JAMES J. KLINK

New York, New York
January 1980

Contents

Construction: Completed Contract Method. Cost-Incurred
Method. Initiation and Support of Operations: Stated Support.
Implied Support. Profit Recognition Where There Is Stated or
Implied Support. Partial Sales: Sale of an Interest in Property.
Seller Has Equity Interest in the Buyer

Condominium Association. Accounting Background. Criteria
for Profit Recognition. Time of Sale. Buyer's Investment in
Purchased Property. Seller's Continued Involvement with
Property Sold. Additional Criteria Established Specifically for
Use of the Percentage of Completion Method. Methods of
Accounting for Profit Recognition: Closing Method. Percentage
of Completion Method. Condominium Conversions. Estimated
Future Costs to Complete. Revisions of Estimated Future Costs.
Sales Subject to Land Lease

Construction Contracts: Methods of Accounting. Percentage of
Completion Method. Completed Contract Method. Provision for
Losses. Sales of Retail Land: Scope of Retail Land Guide.
Criteria for Recording a Sale. Criteria for Accrual Method.
Accounting Procedures—Accrual Method. Interest Rate.
Delinquency and Cancellation. Deferral of Revenues Related to
Future Performance. Accounting Procedures—Installment
Method. Change to Accrual Method from Installment Method.
Sales Subject to Land Lease: Down Payment Test. Computation
of Profit. Sale of an Option: Sale of Option by Option Holder.
Sale of Option by Property Owner. Sales to Limited
Partnerships. Accounting for Nonmonetary Transactions.
Income Tax Considerations

Deposit Method: Accounting Procedures. Provision for Loss.
Nonrecourse Debt Exceeds Net Carrying Value. Recording a
Sale. Forfeiture of Deposit. Installment Method: Accounting
Procedures. Application of Installment Method when Debt Is

Assumed by the Buyer. Wrap-around or All-inclusive Mortgage.
Financial Statement Presentation. Change from Installment
Method to Full Accrual Method. Cost Recovery Method:
Accounting Procedures. Financial Statement Presentation.
Change from Cost Recovery Method to Full Accrual Method.
Financing Method: Accounting Procedures. Lease Method:
Loan to Buyer. Seller Has Option or Obligation to Repurchase.
Profit Sharing (or Co-venture) Method: Accounting Procedures

PART THREE   ACCOUNTING FOR INVESTMENTS IN REAL ESTATE VENTURES

Venture Characteristics. Venture Participants. Legal Form of
Venture. Accounting Background: Accounting Principles Board
Opinion No. 18–1971. AICPA Accounting Guide: Accounting
for Profit Recognition on Sales of Real Estate–1973. Investor
Accounting for Real Estate Joint Ventures. AICPA Statement of
Position 78–9–1978

Investor Accounting for Income and Losses: Controlling
Investor–Consolidate. Noncontrolling Investor–Equity Method.
Equity Method Versus Cost Method. Accounting Principles
Used by the Venture. Varying Profit Participations for
Accounting Purposes. Special Accounting Problems Related to
Recognition of Losses: Recognition of Losses in Excess of an
Investor's Investment. Recognition of Losses in Excess of
Investor's Proportionate Share. Loss in Value of Investment

Capital Contributions: Cash Contributions. Contribution of Real
Estate. Contribution of Services or Intangibles. Investor
Accounting for Interest Income on Loans and Advances to a
Venture: Substance of Loan is a Capital Contribution. Substance
of Loan Is Not a Capital Contribution. Sales of Real Estate to
the Venture. Sales of Services to the Venture. Venture Sells
Real Estate or Services to Investor

Chapter 1

An Overview of the Real Estate Industry

The real estate industry is very large and complex, involving a variety of corporations, partnerships, trusts, and individuals that have different functions and objectives. A profile of the industry would include investors, developers, builders, contractors, brokers, agents, managers, advisors, mortgage lenders and governmental regulators. They may be involved with undeveloped land, single family and multifamily housing, office buildings, shopping centers, industrial buildings, hotels and motels, mobile home parks, resorts or recreational complexes. Generally real estate operations are spread over a large geographical area, although there is some concentration in certain growth communities.

Real estate is now the third largest industry in the United States with approximately 400,000 construction firms and 160,000 real estate service and financing entities. These 560,000 establishments employ approximately 4.3 million workers and account for $300 billion of the gross national product. Traditionally, this industry has been dominated by the small private builder. However, some 300 of the "Fortune 500" companies have been involved in real estate investment or development.

THE INDUSTRY IN THE 1970s

During the last decade, the real estate industry has undergone substantial change. The significant growth of real estate investment trusts, along with the expansion of the economy in the early 1970s, made an excessive supply of funds available for development and construction. The desire and need to invest these funds spurred the rapid expansion of the real estate

1

industry. Large-sçale developments started in numerous areas. Previously, many developers had considered these developments to be too high an investment risk.

As a result of this high activity level, in the mid 1970s construction materials and money supplies became critically short. Inflation rose to a new peacetime high. Interest rates soared to unprecedented high levels. Shortages and rising prices also developed in gasoline and other energy sources. To complicate matters even more, the activities of ecological interest groups, both public and governmental, resulted in substantial delays for many developments. Some buyers had a difficult time obtaining financing. Sales dropped sharply. Contractors were no longer economically able to fulfill their long-term contracts or commitments. All these factors nearly brought development and construction to a stop. The number of foreclosures and bankruptcy filings rose.

In the late 1970s, however, the real estate market recovered impressively. Many projects that had been suspended for months—even years—were completed and sold or rented. Numerous new projects were started, although lenders generally favored low-risk projects, prime locations and developers with proven track records. Many resort developments, however, continued to have problems and some partially completed projects remained dormant.

As the decade neared its close, the high cost of construction coupled with onerous governmental zoning and environmental regulations continued to hamper development. Inflation and high interest rates, which exceeded the record highs of 1974, also cast uncertainty on the future.

The 1970s typified the ups and downs that the real estate roller coaster has always followed. More peaks and valleys can probably be expected in the future.

PROFILE OF THE INDUSTRY

While the industry includes many different activities, the most important are described below.

Investors.   Acquire either (a) land for future appreciation or (b) income producing properties for current income or for cash flow as well as anticipated future appreciation. Income producing properties comprise office buildings, shopping centers, apartments, industrial buildings, hotels, motels, and similar properties rented to others.

Developers. Acquire land and create improvements for their own use or for sale to others. Activities range from subdividing lots for sale to builders, investors, or future homeowners, to commercial development and sale to users or investors.

Merchant Builders. Develop land and sell it for residential or commercial use. They also construct residential or commercial buildings for sale. Most merchant builders are home builders—single family or multifamily— but many are also involved in commercial development and sale.

Investment Builders. Construct income producing properties. They usually intend to hold the property for a long period of time as an investment property.

Contractors. Construct buildings for others at a fixed price or a cost plus fee arrangement. Contractors generally do not own the land or the building.

Mortgage Lenders. Provide short-term loans for acquisition of land as well as development and construction. They also provide long-term loans for permanent financing. The real estate serves as collateral for the loan. Frequently, such loans are secured solely by the real estate and not the full faith and credit of the borrower. Such loans, typically referred to as "nonrecourse loans," limit the creditor's recovery in the event of default solely to the real estate collateralizing the debt.

Brokers. Negotiate as agents for the buyer or the seller in the purchase or sale of real estate. They typically receive commissions as compensation.

TAX SHELTERS

Investments in tax shelters are a very significant source of equity financing in the real estate industry. It is a major factor in many development projects.

Some investors put money in real estate only after carefully considering the effect on their income taxes. Since cash flow may, in part, be nontaxable, tax shelters can result from the excess of the noncash tax deductible expense—depreciation—over the cash required for debt amortization, which is not deductible. And since real estate investments are highly leveraged, debt amortization may almost equal total depreciation over a property's entire life. However, patterns are reversed. Accelerated depreciation is frequently used. It is high in the early years, but decreases over the life of the property. On the other hand, debt amortization usually increases over the term of the debt.

As long as the depreciation exceeds the debt amortization, the investor has a tax shelter. This can even exceed cash flow before mortgage amortization and provide a shelter against tax on other income. The tax savings are, of course, temporary. The tax shelter disappears when the annual debt amortization exceeds the depreciation and the investor's taxable income exceeds his cash flow. At this point, the investor will usually want to sell the property or refinance it to start the process again. A gain on the sale of the property will be taxed at ordinary rates to the extent of depreciation recapture and at capital gains rates on the balance. From a tax standpoint, it may be more desirable to refinance the property. The proceeds of the refinancing are not taxable and the interest portion of the new debt service requirement will result in additional tax deductions.

LEGAL FORMS OF OWNERSHIP

Many real estate entities are comprised of two or more types of owners, usually including developers and investors. The developer generally organizes the entity contributing only a little money, but he may contribute land and receives either fees or part of the profits for his services. The investor contributes money and typically desires cash flow, tax shelter, appreciation, and limited liability. Due to the local nature of most developments, separate entities are often formed for each project. Although many forms of ownership have been used, the most common are listed here.

Corporation. An arrangement whereby each owner has shares of stock evidencing ownership, which can be transferred with relative ease. The corporate firm usually provides legal protection from exposure to liability. Corporate ownership can be convenient for raising funds. The disadvantages of incorporation are that both earnings to the corporation and dividends to the investor are taxed. Tax losses cannot ordinarily be passed through to investors. Joint ventures are sometimes organized as corporations. The ownership of a corporate joint venture seldom changes, though, and its stock is usually not traded publicly.

General Partnership.　An association in which each partner has unlimited liability. Each partner usually has significant influence over the business and assumes joint and several liability for all partnership debts. General partnerships used in connection with specific projects are often called *joint ventures.*

Limited Partnership.　An association in which one or more general partners have unlimited liability and one or more partners have limited liability. This is a very common form of real estate ownership. The limited partnership typically is managed by the general partner, subject to limitations imposed by the partnership agreement. The limited partners generally are passive investors and are not involved in the day-to-day operations. The partnership agreement allocates tax deductions and cash flow to closely match the needs of the developer and investors. Limited partnerships are often called "syndicates." Frequently, developers act as syndicators and sell limited partnership interests to a small group of investors. Sales of large numbers of limited partnership interests usually require registration with the Securities and Exchange Commission (SEC).

Sole Proprietorship.　A form of ownership by one person that offers the obvious advantages of complete control but the disadvantages of complete liability. Any tax losses generated may benefit the owner but often cannot be fully utilized.

Investment Trust.　A corporation or an unincorporated association which ordinarily would be taxed as a corporation. However, trusts meeting the requirements of Sections 856 through 860 of the Internal Revenue Code are permitted a deduction for dividends paid and the amounts thus distributed (including capital gains) are taxable only to the beneficial owner. This benefit can be obtained only if the trust qualifies under an extremely complex set of tax provisions. The more important aspects of these provisions are briefly summarized here:

- At least 100 or more persons must hold beneficial ownership and five or fewer shareholders may not own more than 50 percent of the trust shares.
- The trust must meet income requirements and asset diversification tests which, in general, require the trust to be principally involved in investing in real estate assets (loans and equity interests).
- The trust must be passive in nature and cannot operate property or hold property for sale in the ordinary course of business or it will be subject to a 100 percent tax on the net income from such property. Certain exceptions are made for foreclosure properties.
- At least 95 percent of its ordinary taxable income must be distributed. Only the undistributed portion is taxable to the trust if all the tests are met.

TYPES OF PROJECTS

Real estate projects are generally characterized as residential, commercial or industrial. The more common projects are described below.

Single Family Housing.   Could be either detached or connected, such as duplexes or townhouses. Single family housing also includes condominiums described later. Subdivisions are the typical neighborhood residential developments, usually locally financed. The area is platted, streets are cut and utilities and sewers brought to the lots. Many subdivisions establish architectural controls and use protective covenants. Some of the larger subdivisions have community associations, amenities and school sites. Some developers are only involved with the subdivision of homesite lots from a larger tract and not the construction of homes. They ordinarily sell to builders or individuals.

Condominiums.   Are multifamily structures. The owner of a condominium holds title to his individual dwelling unit. The common areas and amenities are owned jointly with other purchasers in the project. This enables individual mortgages, individual tax assessments and individual unit resales. Condominiums appeal to those seeking the traditional advantages of home ownership with tax savings and potential appreciation and the added advantage of freedom from maintenance of common areas. In a condominium community the homeowners' association is responsible for site maintenance, landscaping, maintenance of the swimming pool and other recreational facilities, entrance lobbies, elevators, halls and roofs. Each individual owner is assessed a monthly charge by the association which is an obligation under the terms of the deed. The homeowners' association is usually set up initially by the developer and later turned over to the individual homeowners.

Condominiums began to gain wide acceptance in 1961 when the National Housing Act was amended to extend government issuance of mortgages to condominiums. By 1968, all fifty states had passed condominium legislation. The real estate boom of the early 1970s saw a dramatic overbuilding of condominiums in certain resort areas.

Apartments. Are multifamily units that are usually either high-rise buildings or the popular low-rise garden-type units. Apartment units are leased to individuals for terms ranging from one month to many years and generally offer the same amenities as condominiums since they are frequently the same type of structure. Unlike other types of income properties, such as shopping centers, very little leasing occurs prior to completion of a building. Significant negative cash flows, therefore, are usually experienced during the initial rent-up period of an apartment, particularly when demand is weak. Because of large operating cost increases and rent controls, owners have had difficulty in obtaining rent increases that keep pace with rising operating costs.

Since there has been increased demand for home ownership, many rental apartment houses are now being converted to condominiums. Some real estate companies specialize in condominium conversions.

Retail Land Projects. Are a unique area of land development that includes the acquisition of large tracts of unimproved land for subdivision into lots. These lots are then for sale to widely dispersed retail customers through intensive marketing programs. Typically, the retail land sale is made with very little down payment required and the balance of the purchase price is paid over a long time period. The lots could be used as a primary or secondary homesite or as recreational property. These lots have frequently been purchased as a speculative investment. Usually these projects include many amenities offered by condominiums, as well as golf courses, marinas and other attractions. It is not uncommon that construction on a purchased lot cannot begin for several years because the necessary site improvements—such as utilities and roads—will not be completed until then. Additionally, promised amenities may not be planned for completion until some time far in the future.

Planned Unit Developments (PUD).   Are land development projects planned as a whole. Dwelling units are grouped into clusters allowing a significant amount of land for open spaces and amenities. A simple PUD may contain a number of similar houses combined with common open space. A complex PUD may include a variety of housing types—detached single family houses, garden apartments, townhouse condominiums—together with open spaces and amenities such as a swimming pool, tennis courts and a community center.

Office Buildings.   Require proper site selection and control of construction costs. An active leasing program is particularly critical to the success of an office building. Mid-term leases—say, for 10 to 15 years—are common for major leases. Leasing usually begins well before the completion of construction and is normally handled by professional agents. Often lenders require that major tenants be obtained before they grant financing. On initial leases, builders frequently are involved with tenant improvements such as interior walls, flooring, and finished carpentry.

Shopping Centers.   Usually depend on a few major tenants with long-term leases. Major tenants such as department stores and supermarkets are referred to as "anchor tenants" and are usually signed up before construction starts. Most shopping center leases include "equity kickers" that provide for additional rents when tenants' sales exceed specified levels. Major shopping centers—such as regional centers or malls—are most often constructed by larger developers who specialize in this type of development. Due to the long lead time in planning, leasing and completion, financing is arranged in advance. Neighborhood or smaller shopping centers are frequently built by developers who are involved in numerous other kinds of development.

Industrial Buildings.   Are generally low-rise structures, such as factories and warehouses, with problems similar to those of office buildings.

Leases of industrial buildings are frequently for a longer term than they are for office buildings. Pre-leasing is very important to success. Industrial buildings sometimes are constructed to meet the needs of a single tenant.

Mobile Home Parks. Are often viewed as temporary users of land in outlying areas pending future development for other uses. It frequently is difficult to obtain zoning for parks due to local opposition. Many mobile home parks are constructed with amenities similar to condominiums. Mobile home parks usually have fairly long rent-up periods and the accompanying negative cash flow.

Hotels and Motels. Are distinctively different from other types of commercial property. Hotels are more often included in the hospitality industry rather than the real estate industry but the real estate investor frequently looks at these projects in a manner similar to other commercial property. Management plays a critical role, as the quality may be as important to success as the proper location. The quality of service and effectiveness of cost control are both largely a function of the quality of management. The maximizing of room revenue requires a delicate balancing between room rates and occupancy.

Occupancy levels are affected dramatically not only by room rates, but also by changes in seasons, business cycles, and the amount and quality of competition. In order to be successful, most hotels not only have to maximize room revenue but also run a profitable food and beverage operation.

New Towns. Allocate land to multiple uses including industrial, commercial, residential and school sites. Whereas subdivisions and planned unit developments discussed above are normally built for areas of existing growth trends, new towns will be located further away from major cities in an attempt to alter existing growth patterns.

Future plans of new towns usually include libraries, theaters and additional amenities. If the new town is designated to become a complete city, it will include housing for a mixture of age groups and economic levels to create a work force for the commercial and industrial elements. New towns are very high-risk investments. The front-end cash requirement is large and the sell-out period is very long. These factors severely limit the future prospects of privately financed new towns.

THE PRODUCTION PROCESS

The steps involved in producing a real estate project illustrate some of the concerns that developers must deal with in the normal course of business.

The *preliminary planning stage* usually involves such efforts as market studies to determine general locations for various project types and to evaluate various available sites. Land options may be used to secure potential sites.

The *planning and design stage* involves feasibility studies to determine if the proposed project is viable. Feasibility studies usually include detailed demand analysis, surveys of area prices, soil tests and cash flow projections. Preliminary architectural plans are often prepared. After the developer is satisfied he has a viable project, he acquires the land.

The *development stage* usually begins with such activities as surveys, engineering studies and detailed cost estimates for development and construction. After a contractor is selected and a price agreed upon, a performance bond is frequently obtained from the contractor to ensure that the contractor will complete the project at the amount contracted. Normally, the marketing effort begins well before the completion of construction.

MARKETS

The real estate industry in recent years has been subject to massive shifts in supply and demand. Due to the long lead time in planning, land acquisition, financing, development, construction, and marketing, developers often make errors in forecasting supply and demand. While growth markets stimulate developers to increase their activity, often many get the same idea at the same time and the market becomes overbuilt. For example, even when apartment occupancies are at an all-time high, too many developers may start massive construction that results in an excessive supply. Easily available money also contributes to overbuilding.

Demand for real estate in recent years also has changed. Tight money has restricted sales because buyers were unable to obtain financing. The shortage of energy has had far-reaching effects on the demand for real estate, especially affecting the type of construction, the location in relation to business districts and mass transit routes, and the feasibility of second homes.

The local developer is particularly vulnerable to changes in supply and demand since he has no alternative markets to provide him with any balance or flexibility.

FINANCING THE PROJECT

Financing real estate is a complex process and different types of financing are required for the various stages of development—land acquisition, development, construction—and permanent financing of the completed project. Due to the complexities of financing and the numerous alternative sources of it, many developers engage brokers or mortgage bankers to assist in obtaining funds.

Common sources of financing are mortgage banks, commercial banks, insurance companies, savings and loan associations, mutual savings banks, governmental agencies (such as HUD), and real estate investment trusts.

The degree of restraint exercised by lenders in granting loans has depended largely on the supply of available money. In the early 1970s many ill-conceived projects were financed. As mentioned earlier, when construction money again became available in the late 1970s, lenders tended to be much more selective, preferring developers with proven track records.

Since most real estate projects are highly leveraged, fluctuations in financing costs usually have a dramatic effect. Interest rates on construction and development loans tend to be based on the risk involved. These rates are commonly pegged at one to five percent above prime. The credit crunch, which in 1979 resulted in a prime rate of 15½ percent, caused interest rates on construction and development loans to reach levels that even otherwise sound projects could not afford. Federal regulation of the monetary supply remains one of the most significant impediments to real estate development.

Dealing with lenders is an important and time-consuming part of the development process. Before seeking financing, developers prepare what is commonly known as a "loan package." The loan package includes such data as market and feasibility studies, a site plan, floor plans, photographs, cash flow projections, the developers' qualifications and experience, and a description of the project. When applying to a particular lender, developers usually supplement the loan package with specific information that the lender requires.

After the developer obtains a loan, he must furnish periodic reports to the lender. For example, a construction loan might require some or all of the following:

- Draw requests that detail expenditures and request additional funds;
- Lien waivers from subcontractors relating to work they have performed;
- Inspection reports from independent engineers regarding the status of construction;
- Financial statements of the developer; and
- Reports on the status of sales or leasing.

In addition to this information, there are also a multitude of legal documents associated with the loan.

CONTRACTORS

The real estate depression of the mid 1970s saw not only wide-scale overbuilding but also saw huge cost overruns in many projects. In many cases, the cost overruns were so large that the projects were uneconomical even without decreases in demand.

Ease of entry into the contracting trades has drawn many contractors who lack experience and working capital. During the early 1970s, good contractors were usually in short supply and, therefore, developers often relied on these inexperienced contractors. Frequently, the results were cost overruns, poor quality construction, and missed deadlines. Since the contractors frequently did not qualify for performance bonds, the loss was quickly shifted to the developer. Also, the developers often acted as general contractors, for which they lacked experience.

All of this illustrates the importance for developers to have effective cost control. Much time is required in preparing master plans and estimates, selecting quality contractors, and securing performance waivers and regulatory approvals.

ENVIRONMENTAL PROBLEMS

Government environmental regulations have become one of the greatest problems for developers. Dealing with these regulations is made even more difficult by the proliferation of agencies that provide piecemeal solutions to specific problems as they occur. This situation has resulted in confusion and long delays in obtaining approvals for development plans. A poignant example of piecemeal solutions is the imposition—with little or no warning—of sewer or water moratoria for indeterminate periods. Some of the key federal laws that affect developers are summarized below:

- *National Environmental Policy Act (1969)*

  This legislation resulted in the creation of the Environmental Protection Agency (EPA) and required the filing of environmental impact statements for federally supported projects.

- *Clean Air Act (1970)*

  This act provides the authority to prevent construction of developments that would increase air pollution above prescribed guidelines.

- *Federal Water Pollution Control Act (1972)*

  This law resulted in the creation of state waste treatment management agencies with authority for land-use planning as well as planning for sewerage plant construction.

- *Coastal Zone Management Act (1972)*

  This legislation was designed to encourage local governments to develop coastal resource management programs that give consideration to environmental, recreational, and economic factors.

- *Flood Disaster Protection Act (1973)*

  This act requires the enactment of local laws to restrict development in flood plains.

Much of the federal regulation has the effect of vesting control and land-use planning powers with state governments—powers that traditionally had been delegated to local governments. Enforcement is often accomplished by a threat to withhold federal funds. Several states have also passed laws requiring environmental impact statements for projects funded by state and local governments. As a result, environmental issues have been the subject of much litigation by citizen groups. These lawsuits have slowed or stopped many proposed projects.

Largely because of these regulations, zoning of a property is critical and a request for a change in zoning can result in costly legal processes. In addition to zoning laws, most communities control development and construction through building permits. Also, a developer may be required to dedicate land to the local government for such projects as parks or street widening. Other local regulations of concern may deal with such matters as sewer tap-in fees and water fees.

OVERVIEW

Despite all of the problems mentioned in this chapter, real estate continues to be a highly attractive investment. But because of the complexities of this industry, it is more important than ever to understand the industry as well as the financial accounting and reporting guidelines discussed in this book.

PART ONE

ACCOUNTING FOR COSTS OF REAL ESTATE

Chapter 2

Capitalization and Allocation of Costs

This chapter deals with accounting for costs incurred on all types of land and real estate developments including preacquisition, acquisition, improvement, development, and construction costs, as well as carrying costs, selling and rental costs, and initial rental operations. Thus, this chapter covers accounting for all real estate up to the point of sale or to the point of normal operations for income-producing properties. It does not encompass the subsequent accounting for operations of income-producing properties such as apartment buildings, office buildings, and shopping centers.

The cost accounting problems that the real estate developer encounters can be best illustrated by considering certain peculiar characteristics of the industry such as the extended business cycle, the nature of common costs and the materiality of transactions.

Business Cycle.   It is not uncommon for a large real estate development to have a business operating cycle (the average time intervening between the acquisition of materials or real estate and the final cash realization) that spans a number of years and may include several economic cycles. It is difficult to develop a complete master plan with a high degree of certainty for a real estate project that requires development over a number of years. Master plans for these projects are often revised numerous times before the project is completed.

Common Costs.   The costs incurred frequently involve large dollar amounts and may benefit more than one project within a development or more than one phase within a project. For example, sewage treatment facilities and amenities may benefit all or a major portion of the total

17

development. This communal benefit, coupled with the heterogeneity of development projects, must be weighed in the selection of capitalization and allocation methods.

Materiality of Transactions. Frequently individual sale and purchase transactions are large, sometimes ranging from hundreds of thousands to millions of dollars.

What are the broad accounting concepts? Costs to develop and construct real estate range from "brick and mortar" costs, which clearly should be capitalized, to general administrative costs, which should not be capitalized. There is a broad range of costs between these two extremes that often are difficult to classify.

Judgmental decisions must be made as to whether such costs should be capitalized. *Accounting Principles Board Statement No. 4,* "Basic Concepts and Accounting Principles," sets forth certain pervasive measurement principles concerning the accounting for costs. The *Statement,* in paragraph 147, states:

> Income determination in accounting is the process of identifying, measuring, and relating revenue and expenses of an enterprise for an accounting period. . . . Expenses are determined by applying the expense recognition principles on the basis of relationships between acquisition costs and either the independently determined revenue or accounting periods. To apply expense recognition principles, costs are analyzed to see whether they can be associated with revenue on the basis of cause and effect. If not, systematic and rational allocation is attempted. If neither cause and effect associations nor systematic and rational allocations can be made, costs are recognized as expenses in the period incurred or in which a loss is discerned.

In paragraph 171, the *Statement* goes on to state:

> Historically, managers, investors and accountants have generally preferred that possible errors in measurement be in the direction of understatement rather than overstatement of net income and net assets. This has led to the convention of conservatism, which is expressed in rules . . . such as the rules that inventory should be measured at the lower of cost or market . . .

The above accounting background presents only broad guidelines. Specific guidelines related to the real estate industry are set forth in the following sections where appropriate.

CAPITALIZATION OF COSTS

Little authoritative literature exists that specifically relates to the principles of accounting for capitalization of costs of real estate. A research study by the Canadian Institute of Chartered Accountants, entitled *Accounting for Real Estate Development Operations,* sets forth the general premise that "land development costs are those costs that are directly attributable to the development of land and to its ownership during the period of the development." Additionally, the AICPA *Accounting Guide: Accounting for Retail Land Sales,* states in paragraph 51:

> Costs directly related to inventories of unimproved land or to construction required to bring land and improvements to a saleable condition are properly capitalizable until a saleable condition is reached. Those costs would include interest, real estate taxes and other direct costs incurred during the inventory and improvement periods.

While the propriety of capitalizing certain costs is obvious, other costs are treated inconsistently in practice throughout the real estate industry. In July 1979, the AICPA issued an Exposure Draft of a proposed Statement of Position, "Accounting for Real Estate Acquisition, Development and Construction Costs." The proposed recommendations are either incorporated or noted herein.

This chapter discusses the capitalization of costs categorized as follows:

Preacquisition costs

Land acquisition costs

Land improvement, development and construction costs

Interest costs

Other carrying costs

Indirect project costs

General and administrative expenses

Amenities

Abandonments and changes in use

Selling and rental costs

Initial rental operations

Condominium conversion costs

Preacquisition Costs

There are currently no specific prescribed guidelines with respect to costs incurred prior to the acquisition of real estate. Preacquisition costs may include legal, architectural and other professional fees, salaries, environmental studies, appraisals, marketing and feasibility studies, and soil tests. Some developers expense these costs while others capitalize them. Many believe that costs incurred before either acquiring the property or obtaining an option to acquire the property are exploratory and thus tantamount to research costs. They believe that accounting in this area should be guided by *Statement of Financial Accounting Standards No. 2,* which requires that research costs be expensed as incurred and not deferred to future periods. Therefore, expensing such costs is the most appropriate treatment under the circumstances, since the future benefits are uncertain.

Other developers follow a course of deferring or capitalizing preacquisition costs. The Exposure Draft of the proposed Statement of Position supports this view, but only if the costs are directly identifiable with a specific property and acquisition is probable. This condition requires that the purchaser is actively seeking acquisition of the property and there is no indication that the property is not available for purchase.

Deferred costs should be charged to expense when acquisition of the property is no longer probable or development planning is suspended. Deferred costs should be capitalized as part of the project costs on acquisition of the property.

Land Acquisition Costs

Costs directly related to the acquisition of land should properly be capitalized. These costs include option fees, purchase costs, transfer costs, title insurance, legal and other professional fees, surveys, appraisals, and real estate commissions. The purchase cost may have to be increased or decreased to impute appropriate interest rates on mortgage notes payable. These are either assumed or issued in connection with the purchase, as required under AICPA *Accounting Principles Board Opinion No. 21,* "Interest on Receivables and Payables." As set forth in the first paragraph of the Opinion:

The use of an interest rate that varies from prevailing interest rates warrants evaluation of whether the face amount and the stated interest rate of a note or obligation provide reliable evidence for properly recording the exchange and subsequent related interest.

If imputation from the stated rate to an appropriate rate is necessary, the mortgage note payable should be adjusted to its present value with a corresponding adjustment to acquisition cost. This would be done by discounting all future payments on the note using an imputed rate of interest at the prevailing rate available for similar financing with independent financial institutions.

Land Improvement, Development and Construction Costs

Costs directly related to improvements of the land should properly be capitalized by the developer. They may include the following items:

- Land planning costs, including marketing and feasibility studies, direct salaries, legal and other professional fees, zoning costs, soil tests, architectural and engineering studies, appraisals, environmental studies, and other costs directly related to site preparation and the overall design and development of the project;
- Onsite and offsite improvements, including demolition costs, streets, traffic controls, sidewalks, street lighting, sewer and water facilities, utilities, parking lots, landscaping, and related costs such as permits and inspection fees;
- Construction costs, including engineering and architectural fees, onsite material and labor, direct supervision, permits, and inspection fees;
- Project overhead and supervision, such as field office costs;
- Recreation facilities such as golf courses, clubhouses, swimming pools, and tennis courts (see the section on "Amenities," page 27; and
- Sales center and models, including furnishing (see the section on "Selling and Rental Costs," page 29).

General and administrative costs not directly identified with the project should be accounted for as period costs and expensed as incurred.

Construction activity on a project may be suspended before a project is completed for reasons such as insufficient sales or rental demand. These conditions may indicate an impairment of the value of a project that may require a writedown or an allowance for loss. (See Chapter 3 on "Net Realizable Value.")

Interest Costs

The long-standing debate on capitalization of interest costs has recently been resolved with the issuance in October 1979 of *Statement of Financial Accounting Standards No. 34* (FAS 34), "Capitalization of Interest Cost." As a result of FAS 34, most real estate developers will be required to make changes, some more dramatic than others. This section describes the evolution of accounting for interest costs and explains the new requirements.

The controversy concerned the proper accounting treatment for interest costs incurred in connection with acquisition of land, development, and construction of real estate held for either sale or investment. Proponents of capitalization argued that such interest costs are a necessary cost of the asset, the same as "bricks and mortar" costs. Proponents of charging off interest costs as a period cost argued that interest is solely a financing cost, a cost that varies directly with the capability of a company to finance development and construction through equity funds.

The vast majority of developers have historically capitalized interest. Expensing interest was also recognized as being acceptable in the AICPA *Accounting Guide: Accounting for Retail Land Sales.* The SEC, however, in *Accounting Series Release No. 163,* "Capitalization of Interest by Companies Other Than Public Utilities," prohibited any SEC reporting company, other than a retail land company required to follow the above Accounting Guide, from changing its accounting policy to capitalize interest. Companies that had previously publicly disclosed an accounting policy of capitalizing interest costs could continue to do so. The SEC moratorium on adoption or extension of a capitalization policy has been revoked by *Accounting Series Release No. 272* as companies comply with FAS 34.

New Accounting Standards. FAS 34 requires capitalization of interest cost as part of the historical cost of acquiring assets that need a period of time to be brought to the condition and location necessary for their intended use. The objectives of capitalizing interest are (1) to obtain a measure of acquisition cost that more closely reflects the enterprise's total investment in the asset and (2) to charge a cost that relates to the acquisition of a resource that will benefit future periods against the revenues of the periods benefited. Interest capitalization is not required if its effect is not material.

FAS 34 requires prospective application in fiscal years beginning after December 15, 1979 and prohibits retroactive adjustment for previously issued financial statements.

Assets Qualifying for Interest Capitalization.   Qualifying assets include real estate constructed for an enterprise's own use or real estate intended for sale or lease. Capitalization is not permitted, however, for assets in use or ready for their intended use or for assets not undergoing the activities necessary to prepare them for use. Thus, land that is not undergoing activities necessary for development is not a qualifying asset for purposes of interest capitalization. If activities are undertaken for developing the land, the expenditures to acquire the land qualify for interest capitalization while those activities are in progress.

Capitalization Period.   The capitalization period commences when:

- Expenditures for the asset have been made;
- Activities that are necessary to get the asset ready for its intended use are in progress; and
- Interest cost is being incurred.

Activities are construed in a broad sense and encompass more than just physical construction. All steps necessary to prepare an asset for its intended use are included. This broad interpretation would include administrative and technical activities during the preconstruction stage, such as developing plans or obtaining required permits.

If substantially all activities related to acquisition of the asset are suspended, interest capitalization should stop until such activities are resumed; however, brief interruptions in activities, interruptions caused by external factors, and inherent delays in the development process would not necessarily require suspension of interest capitalization.

The point at which capitalization of interest should stop was previously not clearly defined in authoritative literature. In the case of raw land, interest was frequently capitalized to the date of sale. This practice is now unacceptable as no interest can be capitalized on land not in the process of development. For projects under development and construction, the predominant practice among developers was to stop capitalization on substantial completion of construction. Nevertheless, capitalization beyond that stage was previously acceptable in some circumstances. Entities capitalizing interest beyond that stage will be required by FAS 34 to change.

Under FAS 34, interest capitalization must end when the asset is substantially complete and ready for its intended use. For projects completed in parts, where each part is capable of being used independently while work continues on other parts, interest capitalization should stop on each part that is substantially complete and ready for use—for example, individual buildings in a multiphase or condominium project. For projects that must be completed before any part can be used, interest capitalization should continue until the entire project is substantially complete and ready for use. Where an asset cannot be used effectively until a particular portion has been completed, interest capitalization would continue until that portion is substantially complete and ready for use—for example, an island resort complex whose sole access is a permanent bridge to the project. Completion of the bridge is necessary for the asset to be used effectively.

Interest capitalization should not stop when the capitalized costs exceed net realizable value. In such instances, a valuation reserve should be recorded or appropriately increased to reduce the carrying value to net realizable value. (See Chapter 3 for net realizable value.)

Methods of Interest Capitalization.   The industry has historically used a number of methods of capitalizing interest. The predominant method was specific identification whereby interest on all debt directly related to the properties was capitalized. Other methods of capitalizing interest were used to a far lesser degree. They involved an allocation of all interest costs to all assets to determine which portion should be capitalized and which portion should be expensed.

Under the new standards, the basic principle is that the amount of interest cost to be capitalized should be the amount that theoretically could have been avoided during the development and construction period if expenditures for the qualifying asset had not been made. These interest costs might have been avoided either by forgoing additional borrowing or by using the funds expended for the asset to repay existing borrowings should no new borrowings be obtained.

The amount capitalized is determined by applying a capitalization rate to the average amount of accumulated capitalized expenditures for the asset during the period. Such expenditures include cash payments, transfer of other assets, or incurrence of liabilities on which interest has been recognized, and should be the net of progress payments received against such capitalized costs. Liabilities, such as trade payables, accruals, and retainages, on which interest is not recognized, are not expenditures. Reasonable approximations of net capitalized expenditures may be used.

The capitalization rate should be based on the rates applicable to borrowings outstanding during the period. Alternatively, if a specific new borrowing is associated with an asset, the rate on that borrowing may be used. If the average amount of accumulated expenditures for the asset exceeds the amounts of specific new borrowings associated with the asset, a weighted average interest rate of all other borrowings must be applied to the excess. Under this alternative, judgment is required to select the borrowings to be included in the weighted average rate so that a reasonable measure will be obtained of the interest cost incurred that could otherwise have been avoided. It should be remembered that the principle is not one of capitalizing interest costs incurred for a specific asset but one of capitalizing interest costs that could have been avoided if it were not for the acquisition, development, and construction of the asset.

The amount of interest cost capitalized in an accounting period is limited to the total amount of interest cost incurred in the period. However, interest cost should include amortization of the premium or discount resulting from imputation of interest on certain types of payables in accordance with *Accounting Principles Board Opinion No. 21,* "Interest on Receivables and Payables," and that portion of minimum lease payments, under a capital lease, that are treated as interest in accordance with FASB *Statement No. 13,* "Accounting for Leases."

Other Carrying Costs. Some developers have historically capitalized other carrying costs, such as real estate taxes and insurance, during the holding, development, and construction periods. Others have expensed these costs. The proposed AICPA Statement of Position indicates that since these costs are similar to interest costs, these other carrying costs should be capitalized only during the period in which interest is permitted to be capitalized. (See page 22.)

Indirect Project Costs

It is generally accepted practice to capitalize indirect project costs that are directly related to the development and construction of real estate projects. The principal problem is defining and identifying the costs to be capitalized. It would be necessary to consider all of the following points before electing to capitalize:

- Specific information should be available (such as timecards) to support the allocation of indirect project costs to specific projects;
- The costs incurred should be incremental costs, that is, in the absence of the project or projects under development or construction, these costs would not be incurred;
- The impact of capitalization of such indirect costs on the results of operations should be consistent with the pervasive principle of matching costs with related revenue; and
- The principle of conservatism should be considered.

Indirect costs directly related to a specific project that should be considered for capitalization include, for example, direct and indirect salaries of a field office and utility and insurance costs. Indirect costs that are not directly related to a project should be charged to current operations.

General and Administrative Expenses

Real estate developers incur various types of general and administrative expenses, including officers' salaries, accounting and legal fees, and various office supplies and expenses. Some of these expenses may be closely associated with individual projects, while others are of a more general nature. For example, a developer may open a field office on a project site and staff it with administrative personnel, such as a field accountant. The expenses associated with this field office are directly associated with the project and are therefore considered overhead. On the other hand, the developer may have a number of expenses associated with general office operations that benefit numerous projects and for which specifically identifiable allocations are not reasonable or practicable. Those administrative costs that cannot be clearly related to projects under development or construction should be charged to current operations.

Amenities

Real estate developments often include amenities such as golf courses, utilities, clubhouses, swimming pools, and tennis courts. The accounting for the costs of these amenities should be based upon management's intended disposition. Note that the author's views concerning the accounting in the event of separate sale or retention of the amenity by the developer, as described in this paragraph, are different from those expressed in the exposure draft, as described in the next paragraph.

- *Amenities sold or transferred with sales units*—all costs in excess of anticipated proceeds, including estimated future losses before sale or transfer to be borne by the developer, should be included in the project costs and allocated as common costs to the cost of sales upon the sale of the related units.

- *Amenities to be sold separately*—costs should be capitalized to the extent of the present value of anticipated proceeds on the sale. Costs, including estimated operating losses prior to the sale, in excess of the present anticipated proceeds, should be charged to project costs and allocated to the cost of sales upon the sale of the related units.

- *Amenities to be retained by developer*—the portion of the costs incurred in developing amenities that are not expected to provide a return sufficient to recover the costs of both operation and construction should be allocated to the cost of sales upon the sale of the related units (after giving effect to the present value of amounts obtainable from operations, future sales, recovery, or salvage).

The accounting for costs of amenities to be sold separately or retained by the developer suggested above is consistent with the AICPA *Accounting Guide: Accounting for Retail Land Sales*. The Exposure Draft of the proposed Statement of Position (SOP) mentioned earlier in this section is not consistent with this position and does not apply in circumstances when that guide applies. The proposed SOP recommends that, when amenities are sold separately or retained by the developer, capitalizable costs in excess of estimated fair value of the amenity on the expected date of substantial physical completion should be allocated as common costs. Under this position, actual operating losses incurred prior to substantial completion should be allocated as common costs. Operating income and losses after substantial completion should be included in current operating results.

Common costs should be allocated based on relative current market value (before construction) of each land parcel benefited. Land parcels benefited should exclude land not expected to be developed in the reasonably near future.

Abandonments and Changes in Use

In the event of abandonment (a foreclosure or lapse of option on real estate), capitalized costs, including allocated common costs related to the real estate developer, should be written off currently and not allocated to other projects or project components.

If there are changes in the intended use of a real estate project (or portion thereof), the write-off may be limited as follows:

1. If changes are pursuant to formal plans for a "higher and better use," the write-off may be limited to the extent that total capitalizable costs incurred and to be incurred exceed the estimated value of the revised project (or portion thereof) at the date of substantial physical completion.
2. If no formal plans exist, the write-off may be limited to the extent such costs exceed the estimated net realizable value of the property, based upon the assumption that it will be sold in its present state.

Selling and Rental Costs

The AICPA issued *Statement of Position 78–3* in June 1978 on real estate start-up costs including costs to sell and rent real estate projects, and initial rental operations of real estate projects. In the absence of contrary evidence, the owner's representation that the project is held for sale or held for rental should govern the accounting to be followed. In rare situations where a portion of the project is held for sale and another portion is held for rental, the costs of the project should be allocated to the separate portions and each portion should be accounted for on a separate project basis.

Selling Costs

The following considerations help determine the appropriate accounting for project selling costs:

Project Costs.　Cost incurred to sell real estate projects should be accounted for in the same manner as, and classified with, construction costs of the project when they meet both of the following criteria:

- The costs incurred are for tangible assets which are used throughout the selling period or for services performed to obtain regulatory approval for sales; and
- The costs are reasonably expected to be recovered from sales of the project or incidental operations.

The cost of model units, related furnishings, sales facilities, certain legal fees and similar costs, and semipermanent signs meet these criteria.

Prepaid Expenses.　Costs, other than project costs, that are incurred to sell real estate projects should be accounted for and classified as prepaid expenses when they are incurred for goods or services before the related goods are used or before the services are performed.

Examples of prepaid expenses are expenditures for future advertising, sales brochures, and commission advances.

Certain prepaid expenses, such as sales commissions that are identifiable with specific future revenue, should be charged to operations in the period in which the related sales revenue is earned. Other prepaid expenses that are not identifiable with specific future revenues should be charged to expense during the period of expected benefit.

Period Costs.　Costs that are incurred to sell real estate projects, but that do not meet the criteria for project costs or prepaid expenses, should be charged to expenses as incurred. Examples of expenditures that are period costs are those incurred for media advertising, sales salaries and overhead, and grand openings.

Rental Costs

The following considerations help determine the appropriate accounting for project rental costs.

Chargeable to Future Periods. Costs incurred to rent real estate projects should be charged to future periods when they are prepaid expenses (see above), or when they are associated with future revenue and their recovery is reasonably expected.

Examples of costs that meet the criteria for deferral are expenditures for commissions, model units and related furnishings, rental facilities, semipermanent signs, and brochures.

Deferred rental costs that can be directly related to specific leases should be amortized over the term of the related lease. Deferred rental costs that cannot be directly related to specific leases should be amortized to expense over the period of expected benefit. Estimated unrecoverable deferred rental costs should be written off when it is probable the lease will be terminated.

Period Costs. Costs that are incurred to rent real estate projects which do not meet the above criteria should be charged to expenses as incurred. Examples of expenditures that are period costs are media advertising, rental salaries and overhead, and grand openings.

Initial Rental Operations

Established industrial and commercial companies generally expense initial operating and start-up costs in the period incurred. However, in an attempt to achieve a better matching of costs and revenue, certain real estate companies defer start-up costs and initial operating losses. The accounting treatment often varies, depending on the purpose and amount of the expenditures, as well as the anticipated future benefits and revenue. Typically, the deferral of such costs and losses has stopped when a specific event takes place—such as the initiation of an active sales program, attainment of a certain level of occupancy, or expiration of a predetermined period of time. Of course, start-up and preoperating costs that are not expected to be recovered from future revenue should not be deferred.

The aforementioned AICPA *Statement of Position 78–3* on accounting for selling and rental costs also covers accounting for initial rental operations of real estate projects. It states that certain costs incurred during construction, before a rental project is capable of producing revenue, should be capitalized. That practice is supported by ample precedent but, once major construction activity is completed and the project is capable of producing revenue, the accounting for costs and revenue should reflect the change in status of the project.

As defined in the *Statement of Position,* a rental project is "substantially completed and held available for occupancy" if it meets both of the following conditions:

- Construction has reached the stage at which the builder originally intended to cease major construction activity; and
- Units are being or have been offered for rental.

The *Statement of Position* concludes that at that stage, a change in the status of the rental project has taken place and the owner's principal activities are substantially different from those during the construction stage.

Accounting for initial operations of a rental project that is substantially completed and held available for occupancy should follow the procedures listed here:

- Rental revenue should be recorded in income as earned;
- Operating costs should be charged to expense currently;
- Amortization of deferred rental costs should begin;
- Full depreciation of rental property should begin; and
- Carrying costs, such as interest and property taxes, should be charged to expense as accrued.

Condominium Conversion Costs

The conversion of rental property to condominiums has become common in the last few years in many areas of the country. This trend has been caused by rent controls, rising real estate taxes, and increased operating and maintenance costs that have reduced the return on rental operations and, in many instances, created operating losses. Property owners have, in several instances, either sold the property to a condominium convertor or directly converted the property to condominiums both to halt operating losses and maximize sales proceeds upon liquidation.

Conversion Costs.   Direct costs incurred in conversion are properly capitalized. They may include:

- Cost of renovation and construction to upgrade the property, including a warranty reserve where applicable;
- Cost of financing during the conversion period—including interest costs on the cost of renovation and construction;
- Legal and printing costs associated with producing the condominium documents;
- Commitment fees paid to obtain commitments from lending institutions to provide financing for purchasers; and/or
- Assessments on unsold units paid to condominium association.

Debt Prepayment Penalties.   Often it is necessary to refinance the property prior to conversion because the original permanent loan does not provide for the release of liens on a unit basis. Such refinancing may result in a prepayment penalty. It would appear that this cost is a cost of conversion and properly capitalizable in a manner similar to interest during construction, but the accounting principle for this type of transaction is set forth in AICPA *Accounting Principles Board Opinion No. 26,* "Early Extinguishment of Debt":

> The Board concludes that all extinguishments of debt before schedule maturities are fundamentally alike. The accounting for such transactions should be the same regardless of the means used to achieve the extinguishment. . . . A difference between the reacquisition price and the net carrying amount of the extinguished debt should be recognized currently in income of the period of extinguishment as losses or gains and identified as a separate item. . . . Gains and losses should not be amortized to future periods.

The appropriate accounting for the prepayment penalty varies depending upon the circumstances. If the conversion is made by the owner who operated the property as a rental operation, the prepayment penalty should be charged to expense of the rental operations in the period incurred. The penalty is in essence an adjustment to the interest charged to past periods.

If material in amount, the penalty should be classified as an extraordinary loss, net of the related income tax effect. If, however, conversion is made by a convertor who acquired the property as inventory, the prepayment penalty may be capitalized to the property account. In this case, the prepayment penalty is normally one of the factors taken into consideration in determining the price paid by the convertor.

Results of Rental Operations.   During the conversion period, revenues are often lost from leases not being renewed, as happens when tenants do not purchase their apartments and subsequently move out. As in the case of prepayment penalties, the accounting for the results of rental operations varies depending upon the circumstances.

If conversion is made by the owner who operated the property as a rental operation, the owner is often attempting to halt operating losses from rental operations through conversion of the property. Where the owner is directly converting the property, results of rental operations during the conversion period should continue to be reflected in the income statement in the period incurred. If, however, conversion is made by a convertor who acquired the property as inventory, the anticipated loss from rental operations during the conversion period is normally one of the factors taken into consideration in determining the price paid by the convertor to acquire the property. Therefore, the net loss from rental operations in these circumstances can be capitalized.

ALLOCATION OF COSTS

After it has been determined what costs are capitalized, it then becomes important to determine how the costs should be allocated. These costs will enter into the calculation of cost of sales of individual units. Although different methods of allocation can be used in different circumstances, judgment must often be used to ascertain that appropriate results are obtained.

Costs to Be Allocated

Regardless of the size of a real estate development, the capitalized costs can be summarized as one of the following:

- Common to the entire development;
- Common to only certain segments or projects within the development;
- Related directly to construction of buildings being sold; or
- Related directly to the individual sales transaction.

The first two types of costs must be allocated in an appropriate manner with individual sales transactions. The last two types should be specifically charged to the property being sold since they are directly related.

Methods of Cost Allocation

With respect to allocation of capitalized costs, the only specific source in accounting literature is the AICPA *Accounting Guide: Accounting for Retail Land Sales,* which describes three methods frequently used in practice: *specific identification, value,* and *area.* It further states that any of these methods, consistently applied, may be used. The method used to allocate costs should accomplish the objective of matching costs with related revenue. The guide applies only to retail land companies and does not provide any precision as to when each method may be appropriate.

The author believes that specific identification should be used to the extent practicable. For common costs, the value method should normally be used as it is less likely to result in deferral of losses. This is consistent with the Exposure Draft of the proposed AICPA *Statement of Position,* "Accounting for Real Estate Acquisition, Development, and Construction Costs." Descriptions of the methods used follow.

Specific Identification Method.   This method of cost allocation is based on determining actual costs applicable to each parcel of land. It is rarely used for land costs because such costs usually encompass more than one parcel. It is frequently appropriate, however, for direct construction costs because these costs are directly related to the property being sold. This method should be used whenever practicable.

Value Method.   The value method is the one predominantly used. With this method, the allocation of common costs should be based on relative current values (before direct improvement costs) of each land parcel benefited. In multiproject developments, however, common costs are normally allocated based on estimated sales prices net of direct construction and selling costs. This approach is usually the most appropriate because it is less likely to result in deferral of losses.

An example illustrating the use of the value method to allocate common costs for a condominium project that consists of three buildings, each being defined as an individual "project" for accounting purposes is set forth in Table 2.1.

Area Method. This method of cost allocation is based upon square footage, acreage or frontage. The use of this method does not usually result in a logical allocation of costs. When negotiating the purchase price for a large tract of land, the purchaser considers the overall utility of the tract, recognizing that various parcels in the tract are more valuable than others. For example, parcels on a lake front are usually more valuable

Table 2.1.   Allocation of Common Costs Under the Value Method

	Project		
	A	*B*	*C*
Number of units	75	75	100
Estimated sales value	$2,600,000	$3,200,000	$4,200,000
Less: direct improvement and selling costs	1,800,000	2,300,000	3,500,000
Sales value net of direct costs (aggregate of $2,400,000)	$ 800,000	$ 900,000	$ 700,000
Allocation of common costs aggregating $1,500,000:			
1,500,000 × 800,000/2,400,000	500,000		
1,500,000 × 900,000/2,400,000		562,500	
1,500,000 × 700,000/2,400,000			437,500
Gross profit	$ 300,000	$ 337,500	$ 262,500
Percent of sales	11.5%	10.5%	6.2%
Had the value method been applied based on gross sales value, the results would have been:			
Allocation of common costs	$ 390,000	$ 480,000	$ 630,000
Gross profit	410,000	420,000	70,000
Percent of sales	15.8%	13.1%	1.7%

than those back from the lake. In this situation, if a simple average based
on square footage or acreage were used to allocate costs to individual
parcels, certain parcels could be assigned costs in excess of their net realizable value.

Generally, the use of the area method should be limited to situations
where each individual parcel is estimated to have approximately the same
reative value. Under such circumstances, the cost allocations, as determined by either the area or value methods, would be approximately the
same.

Revision of Cost Allocations and Estimates

Costs should generally be revised and reallocated on the basis of current
estimates of costs and relative values. Changes in estimates should be applied prospectively in current and future periods, except as follows. When
sales of real estate are recorded, it may be necessary to accrue certain
estimated costs not yet incurred. Adjustments of accruals for costs applicable to sales previously recognized in full, where deferral for future
performance was not required, should be recognized in the current period.

Chapter 3

Net Realizable Value

Accounting for net realizable value of real estate held for sale has received considerable attention in recent accounting literature. On May 25, 1976, the AICPA issued for public comment an Exposure Draft of a proposed Statement of Position entitled "Valuation of Real Estate and Loans and Receivables Collateralized by Real Estate." The proposed statement concluded that real estate inventory should not be carried at an amount in excess of its estimated net realizable value (NRV), which is determined by an evaluation of the recoverability of the individual property.

Net realizable value should, according to the statement, be based on the estimated selling price plus other estimated revenue from the property during the expected holding period, reduced by:

1. the estimated cost to complete or improve such property to the condition used in determining the estimated selling price;
2. the estimated costs to dispose of the property; and
3. the estimated costs to hold the property to the expected point of sale, including future interest, property taxes, legal fees, and other direct holding costs. Estimated interest holding costs should be based on the higher of
   (a) the average cost of all capital (debt and equity); or
   (b) the entity's accounting policy for capitalizing interest.

There has been considerable controversy about whether future interest costs to hold real estate should be considered in determining NRV.

In June 1979 the AICPA prepared an Issues Paper covering the same subject matter. It has been sent to the Financial Accounting Standards Board to see if it will place the subject on its agenda. The AICPA plans to publish the Statement of Position, pending the decision of the FASB on its disposition. Until a position paper is formally issued, the following guidelines are appropriate.

General Principles

Real estate held for sale, or for development and sale, should be included in the balance sheet at the lower of cost or market. This principle is one of long standing; however, the decline in real estate values in the mid 1970s has brought the application of this general principle sharply into focus for many companies.

Accounting Research Bulletin No. 43, Chapter 4, "Inventory Pricing," states:

> the term market means current replacement cost (by purchase or by production . . .) except that:
> 1. Market should not exceed the net realizable value (that is estimated selling price in the ordinary course of business less reasonably predictable costs of completion and disposal), and
> 2. Market should not be less than net realizable value reduced by an allowance for an approximately normal profit margin.

Major questions about the application of the above principles are:

- What types of real estate should be regarded as inventory and what types should be regarded as long-term investment?
- Should the principle of lower of cost or net realizable value be applied to individual items or groups of items?
- Should cost of completion include the cost (especially interest cost) to carry the inventory to date of sale?

Inventory Versus Long-term Investment

It is generally agreed that real estate held for sale, or for development and sale, falls in the category of inventory. Thus the inventory guidelines would cover such properties as land (including raw land and land under development), condominiums and single-family housing, as well as income properties held for sale. Raw land should generally be categorized as inventory because in time it will become inventory. On the other hand, inventories would not include:

- Income properties held for long-term investment;
- Real property used in the business; or
- Land held for development or construction of property held for long-term investment or property used in the business.

For example, an office building used in a company's business would not be considered inventory. On the other hand, if the office building were held for sale or expected to be sold, it would be subject to the above guidelines for inventories.

It is not appropriate for income properties to be declared to be held for investment solely to avoid losses that otherwise would have to be recorded under rules of inventories.

In the evaluation of real estate held for sale or for development and sale, each of the following factors should be considered:

- The company's financial ability to hold or to develop the properties in question;
- The company's plans for the properties, including information about its past practices and experience;
- The company's plans for the timing of development and sale; and
- Appraisals of the property prepared either by independent appraisers or by the company staff.

Individual Item or Group Basis

As a general rule, because of the relatively low volume and high dollars of individual sales transactions in the real estate industry, the lower-of-cost-or-market test should be applied to each individual sales unit, except where the units are relatively homogeneous—such as units in a condominium project. In the latter case, the test may be applied on a project-by-project basis or the group basis.

The group convention was principally established for a manufacturing concern. For the group convention to be appropriate for real estate inventories, there must be a high volume of transactions, with each individual component of the group having approximately the same rate of turnover.

Since this condition is not usually present in the real estate industry, the group convention is not usually appropriate.

Where the developer uses the value method to allocate costs to individual units, net realizable value as determined either on a project-by-project basis or on an individual unit basis should be approximately the same.

Determination of Net Realizable Value

In the application of the general principle of lower of cost or market, the term "market" generally means estimated net realizable value (that is, estimated selling price in the ordinary course of business less costs of completion and disposal). As previously discussed, market should usually be applied on an item-by-item basis rather than a group basis.

Selling Price. The estimated selling price should usually be determined on the basis of a sale in the ordinary course of business, which would allow a reasonable time to find a willing purchaser under normal market conditions, exclusive of any adjustment for estimated inflation. If, however, the intention is to dispose of the property on an immediate sale basis, or if the owner does not have the financial ability to hold the property, the estimated selling price should be determined on an immediate liquidation basis.

The method used to determine estimated selling prices varies depending on the nature of the property. Selling prices on bulk undeveloped land should ordinarily be based on comparable sales prices allowing a reasonable time to find a purchaser. Certain future events, such as prospective scientific developments or possible future legislation, should not be factored into the determination of the estimated selling prices except to the extent that such events are being recognized currently in the marketplace. Possible future zoning should not be considered unless it is reasonably certain it can be obtained.

In determining selling prices for property under development—such as retail lots, single-family homes, and condominiums—current sales prices should be used. Where experience is lacking or where there has been relatively low sales volume, selling prices of comparable transactions in the local area should be used. Although selling prices should not be adjusted for inflation, it would be appropriate in the case of long-term developments when significant development work remains to be completed—such as certain retail land developments—to adjust selling prices for the effect of inflation upon the costs required to complete the work. This would only be appropriate when there is a reasonable assurance that cost increases can be recovered in sales prices on a dollar-for-dollar basis.

Income properties usually are valued on the basis of their estimated future net cash flow and a capitalization rate that may vary with the type of project and the money market. Estimated future cash flow should be based on full or stabilized operations with appropriate reductions for the estimated cash flow shortfalls prior to stabilization. When using such a valuation process to determine estimated selling prices, *pro forma* operating costs should be based on current costs rather than historical averages. For example, future net cash flow should be adjusted to reflect recent increases in utility costs. An example illustrating the calculation of net realizable value (market value using appraisal techniques) for income properties is set forth in Table 3.1.

Table 3.1. Calculation of Net Realizable Value for Income Property

Assumptions
1. An apartment project is currently under construction with a current book value of $2,400,000 and an estimate of $150,000 to complete.
2. It is estimated that rentals will reach a level of stabilization at the end of two years with net cash flow of $300,000 annually.
3. The appropriate capitalization rate for this investment is considered to be 12 percent.
4. The present value of cash flow shortfalls to stabilization is $275,000 and $100,000 in years 1 and 2, respectively.

Calculation of Net Realizable Value	
Estimated net cash flow at stabilization (year 2)	$ 300,000
Capitalization rate	÷ .12
Sales value in 2 years	2,500,000
Less: present value of cash flow shortfalls from stabilized amounts	
year 1	(275,000)
year 2	(100,000)
Estimated costs to complete	(150,000)
Net realizable value (market value)	2,025,000
Current book value	2,400,000
Required reserve	$ 375,000

Cost of Completion (Including Interest and Property Taxes). The total cost of completing properties being evaluated should include all additional costs that will be incurred to complete the property to be sold. These costs should include the effects of inflation and should be determined on a basis consistent with the determination of costs that are capitalizable or included in inventory.

As previously mentioned, there has been considerable controversy as to whether future interest costs should be considered in determining NRV. It has long been the author's view that the future interest costs should be included in the calculation if such interest costs were capitalized as a part of the cost of the project. The Financial Accounting Standards Board issued in October 1979, *Statement of Financial Accounting Standards No. 34* (FAS 34) "Capitalization of Interest Costs," which requires the capitalization of interest cost as part of the historical cost of development and construction of real estate projects. (See the section on interest cost on page 22 for further discussion of FAS 34.) The thrust of FAS 34 is that interest costs during the improvement period should not be treated differently from bricks and mortar. Moreover, paragraph 19 of FAS 34 indicates that capitalization should not stop when accounting principles require recognition of a lower carrying value for the asset. The allowance required to reduce the acquisition cost to a lower carrying value should be established or increased appropriately.

Although FAS 34 does not directly address the question of which, if any, interest costs should be included in the NRV computation, the only logical conclusion from the Statement is that the estimated future capitalizable interest costs should be included in the NRV computation. The controversy, however, has not been resolved over whether to include other future interest costs in determining NRV. Other future interest costs would include such costs until the estimated time of sale with respect to undeveloped land or developed real estate after substantial completion. The author's view is that such additional interest costs should not be included.

The AICPA proposed Statement of Position tentatively concluded that interest costs should be included in the calculation to the estimated date of sale even if interest costs are expensed. However, the proposal was prepared prior to FAS 34. Therefore, it is not determinable as of the end of 1979 what effect FAS 34 will have on the proposal or whether the FASB will address the subject. The reader should be aware that the FASB or the AICPA could take some action after 1979 to resolve the issue of how much interest cost, if any, should be included in the computation.

There have been two approaches generally used to include future interest costs in the calculation of net realizable value. One method, which is consistent with FAS 34, is to include the interest cost in the estimated aggregate cost of the property. To the extent that it exceeds the estimated future sale proceeds, it is recognized currently in the loss provision. Another method indirectly reflects future interest costs by discounting estimated future sales proceeds (net of estimated cash disbursements exclusive of interest) to present value. The resulting amount is compared to costs accumulated to date to determine any loss provision required. Effectively, the former method measures the loss as the difference between total estimated costs to be incurred and estimated proceeds at the future date, whereas the latter measures the loss as the difference in cost and value at a current date. The latter method is illustrated in the Appendices to AICPA *Statement of Position 75–2,* "Accounting Practices of Real Estate Investment Trusts." Although that Statement requires an interest rate based on an average cost of capital (that is, total interest cost divided by the aggregate of debt and equity), it should be noted that the FASB rejected that approach for purposes of interest capitalization in FAS 34.

What about future property taxes during the holding period? If, as a matter of accounting policy property taxes are not capitalized, future property taxes need not be included in the calculation. On the other hand, if property taxes have been capitalized, then property taxes to the estimated date of disposal should be included in the estimated cost of completion. The AICPA proposal has tentatively concluded that property taxes should be included in the computation of NRV even when the accounting policy is to expense such costs.

Costs of Disposal.   These costs should include marketing, selling, advertising, points, fees and commissions.

Reversal of Reserves.   Because of the many factors that can affect recoverability of investments in real estate, the estimated loss on an individual unit or project may not be the same as the ultimate loss sustained on the disposition of the property. Where the valuation is based on estimates, the reduction in value is treated as a valuation reserve that could be adjusted periodically based on a relatively complete reevaluation.

However, if the valuation has been determined based on known losses caused by specific sales contracts or commitments, the property should be written down to net realizable value.

Examples of the Calculation of Net Realizable Value of Bulk Land.
Assume that a real estate developer owns 3000 acres of bulk land that he
plans to develop in the future. To date no commitment for development has been made, although there are a number of possible alternatives. The book value per acre is $1500. The developer expenses interest
in accordance with FAS 34.

Consider these additional facts and the valuation of the land under the
principles we've discussed:

1. One hundred and forty of the 3000 acres have recently been sold
   in bulk for $1500 per acre. The 140 acres are reasonably typical of
   the remaining acreage in character and value. In this situation, it is
   recognized that the 3000 acres may not, or even probably will not,
   be sold immediately or even within a year. In this situation (ignoring
   sales commission for the moment), the sale may be reasonable evidence of "replacement cost" and no reserve or write-down is required. As long as current values are used, no consideration is required for future interest cost to hold the property. Regarding sales
   commissions, it generally will be necessary to consider selling cost
   as a reduction of "replacement cost" when (a) it is expected that
   the property will be sold for the "replacement cost" of $1500 and
   the selling costs will be incurred or (b) the property is held for
   sale.

2. If the sale listed above was not part of the parcel owned, but was
   comparable to the parcel owned, the conclusion should be the
   same.

3. If no sales occurred and competent appraisal techniques lead to the
   conclusion that (a) comparable sales can be made but only after
   three years and (b) no current sales are possible except at clearly
   distressed prices (and there is no expectation of making sales in this
   manner), then the sales value of $1500 (and thus "replacement
   cost") is appropriate after three years. Nevertheless, the conclusion
   is still the same. A reserve is not required as interest cannot be capitalized on land not under development. In view of the proposed
   AICPA position, however, it would be acceptable to provide a reserve for the excess of (a) current net book value of $1500 plus all
   future costs including interest cost based on the average cost of capital less (b) sales value of $1500 per acre.

Note that appraisal techniques frequently result in a deduction of interest based on a risk rate of return during the three years involved in arriving at the valuation. If this is the case, the interest may be added back before making the preceding calculation, which includes the developer's future interest cost for the three years.

PART TWO

ACCOUNTING FOR SALES OF REAL ESTATE

Chapter 4

Accounting Background and Government Regulation

The first authoritative literature specifically related to accounting for profit recognition on sales of real estate was the *Accounting Series Release No. 95* issued by the Securities and Exchange Commission in 1962. Real estate developers, however, encountered various difficulties in the late 1960s and the early 1970s that led to substantial adverse publicity with regard to their accounting and sales practices. In response to the obvious need for better guidelines, the AICPA in 1973 issued two accounting guides, *Accounting for Retail Land Sales* and *Accounting for Profit Recognition on Sales of Real Estate*. The latter accounting guide has since been amended by two Statements of Position on questions concerning profit recognition on sales of real estate and application of alternative methods in accounting for sales of real estate. Some sales of real estate also come under government regulation, such as the Interstate Land Sales Full Disclosure Act and the Securities and Exchange Commission. This chapter sets forth a brief summary of accounting literature and government regulations.

Accounting Series Release No. 95

Accounting Series Release No. 95 included examples of real estate transactions in which the Securities and Exchange Commission deemed it inappropriate to recognize profit at the time of sale. The release indicated that the following circumstances tend to raise a question about the propriety of current recognition of profit:

- Evidence of financial weakness of the purchaser;
- Substantial uncertainty of the amount of costs to be incurred;

- Substantial uncertainty of the amount of proceeds to be realized;
- Retention of effective control of the property by the seller;
- Limitations and restrictions on the purchaser's profits and on the development or disposition of the property;
- Simultaneous sale and repurchase by the same or affiliated interests;
- Concurrent loans to purchasers;
- Small or no down payment; and
- Simultaneous sale and leaseback of property.

This release, which was applicable only to publicly held entities, did not anticipate the diversity and complexity of real estate transactions in the 1960s. As a result, there was a wide variation in practice and many abuses even after the Accounting Series Release was issued. A reevaluation of accounting for real estate transactions became necessary.

AICPA Accounting Guide:
Accounting for Retail Land Sales

In 1970 the AICPA's Committee on Land Development Companies began a review of the accounting and reporting practices of the retail land sales industry—an industry characterized by the retail marketing of numerous lots, subdivided from a larger parcel of land for use as primary or secondary homesites. This review culminated in the issuance of the 1973 AICPA *Accounting Guide: Accounting for Retail Land Sales,* which applies only to retail lot sales on a volume basis. (See Chapter 10 for accounting for sales in this industry.)

AICPA Accounting Guide: Accounting for
Profit Recognition on Sales of Real Estate

In August 1971, the AICPA established the Committee on Accounting for Real Estate Transactions to appraise accounting practices in the real estate industry and to recommend changes. As a result of the committee's deliberations, *Accounting for Profit Recognition on Sales of Real Estate,* hereafter referred to as the *Profit Recognition Accounting Guide,* was issued in 1973. This guide covers the timing of profit recognition for all real estate sale transactions except retail lot sales on a volume basis. Retail lot sales are covered by the previously issued AICPA accounting guide *Ac-*

counting for Retail Land Sales. The *Profit Recognition Accounting Guide* is, therefore, intended to cover sales of lots to builders of homes, condominiums, buildings, parcels of land to builders and others, partial interests in real estate, options and businesses, if most of the assets are real estate.

The committee emphasized that economic substance and not legal form should govern the timing of profit recognition. It determined that the two matters with the greatest impact on the timing of profit recognition are:

- The extent of the buyer's investment in the property required to give reasonable certainty as to collection of the seller's receivable.
- Continuing involvement of the seller with property sold.

The committee then concluded in paragraph 7 that revenues should not be recognized until:

(a) The amount of the revenue is measurable—that is, the collectibility of the sales price is reasonably assured or the amount uncollectible can be estimated—and

(b) The earnings process is complete or virtually complete—that is, the seller is not obliged to perform significant activities after the sale to earn the revenue.

Unless both of these conditions are met, recognition of all or part of revenue and/or profit on a sale transaction is postponed.

Interpretations of the Profit Recognition Accounting Guide have been issued in the form of two AICPA Statements of Position. The first was *Statement of Position 75–6,* "Questions Concerning Profit Recognition on Sales of Real Estate," issued in 1975, which dealt with 12 separate questions relating to the guide. The second was *Statement of Position 78–4,* "Application of the Deposit, Installment, and Cost Recovery Methods in Accounting for Sales of Real Estate," issued in 1978, which dealt with the diverse methods of application of those accounting methods.

The provisions of the *Profit Recognition Accounting Guide* have been generally accepted in practice and, to a large extent, are the basis for the guidelines, interpretations and examples set forth herein.

Interstate Land Sales Full Disclosure Act

The 1968 Interstate Land Sales Full Disclosure Act requires that a land developer, who sells or leases through interstate commerce 50 or more lots of undeveloped land pursuant to a "common promotional plan," must register the land with the Department of Housing and Urban Development (HUD) and make full disclosure concerning the lots to purchasers or lessees. The developer registers by filing a statement of record with HUD's Office of Interstate Land Sales Registration (OILSR) and makes the required disclosure by delivering to the purchaser or lessee, before an agreement is signed, a property report containing certain prescribed items of information. Certain transactions are exempted by the Act from the registration and disclosure requirements.

Contracts for the purchase or lease of lots are voidable at the option of the purchaser or lessee if the lots are not registered, or if the purchaser or lessee has not been furnished with the required property report. In addition, the willful violation by the land developer of the registration and property report delivery requirement of the Act may constitute a criminal offense. Furthermore, the Act permits a person acquiring a lot covered by the Act to recover losses in the value of the lot from the land developer. The buyer must, however, prove that the statement of record or the property report relating to his lot contained an untrue statement of a material fact or failed to state a material fact required to be stated therein, or if other misrepresentations or deceptive practices were used in connection with the sale or lease of the lot.

Regulations promulgated under the Act and the forms prescribed for use in complying with the Act's requirements are set forth in Title 24, Chapter IX of the Code of Federal Regulations.

Financial Statement Requirements.   As noted in the regulations, the financial statements must include a balance sheet, a statement of profit and loss, and a statement of the sources and uses of cash. The statements must be prepared in accordance with generally accepted accounting principles. The statement of record and the property report must contain financial statements. If the aggregate sales price of the lots to be offered is over $500,000 and 300 or more lots are involved, the financial statements must be audited by a Certified Public Accountant or a public accountant.

Applicability to the Condominium Developer.   The regulations on interstate land sales were revised as of December 1, 1973. The definition of a "lot," which was added by the revision and appears in Section 1710.1(h) of the regulations, clarified a position long taken by OILSR that the Act was intended to cover condominium units. A condominium is viewed by OILSR as the equivalent of a subdivision with each unit being a lot, because the right to condominium space is considered to be a form of ownership, not a structural description.

The preamble to the revised regulations, which appeared in the September 4, 1973 Federal Register, stated that Congress recognized the need to exempt professional builders from the Act and provided an appropriate exemption in Section 1403(a)(3) of the Act as follows:

> The provisions of this title shall not apply to . . . the sale or lease of any improved land on which there is a residential, commercial, or industrial building, or to the sale or lease of land under a contract obligating the seller to erect such a building thereon within a period of two years.

The preamble went on to say:

> For a condominium unit sale to be exempted from the Act, it must accordingly qualify for exemption; i.e., either it must be completed before it is sold, or it must be sold under a contract obligating the seller to erect the unit within two years from the date the purchaser signs the contract of sale. For the purposes of the exemption cited, "building" comprises the dwelling unit and all utilities or systems necessary to support normal occupancy. Additionally, if a condominium dwelling unit is merely incidental to the common facilities (as in the case of recreational developments), all common facilities must be completed within the two-year period to qualify for the exemption since frequently vacation sites are sold without assurances that such facilities will be completed. With respect to condominiums intended as primary residences in metropolitan areas, registration typically is unnecessary since most professional builders would qualify for the exemption inasmuch as they are able to deliver a completed unit to a purchaser within two years after the contract of sale has been signed.

Neither the regulations nor the preamble specifically define "recreational condominiums" as opposed to "condominiums intended as primary residences in metropolitan areas," and it is likely that this definitional issue will have to be resolved on a case-by-case basis. If a developer is uncertain about a particular case, it may be prudent to seek an exemption advisory opinion from OILSR.

In early 1974, OILSR issued guidelines to further clarify the applicability of federal land sales registration laws (particularly Section 1403(a)(3)) to the offer and sales of condominiums. These guidelines are as follows:

- The use of exculpatory clauses which excuse performance because of acts of God or material shortages may be included in the contract and will not be viewed as an attempt to gain an exemption without the necessary contractual obligation to complete performance within two years;
- The two-year period will not begin until the buyer signs the contract for sale. The execution of a reservation, with the deposit placed in escrow, will not constitute a sale under the Act as it is only an expression of interest; and
- When the two-year period ends, the unit under contract must be physically habitable. Moreover, the common areas of the condominium, when deemed "the primary inducement to purchase," must also be ready for use by the end of the two-year period.

These guidelines, in all likelihood, will be tested on a case-by-case basis.

Securities and Exchange Commission

Various types of real estate transactions are the equivalent of an offering of securities in the form of an investment contract or a participation in a profit sharing arrangement within the meaning of the Securities Act of 1933 and the Securities Exchange Act of 1934. The more common types of real estate transactions that may require registration under the Securities Act are sales of interests in limited partnerships and condominiums.

The condition under which an offering of condominium units is construed to be an offering of securities is covered in SEC *Securities Acts Release No. 5347.* The release states that certain offers and sales of condominium units that are coupled with an offer or agreement to perform or arrange certain rental or other services for the purchaser may involve the offering of securities in a form of investment contract or a participation in a profit sharing agreement within the meaning of the Securities Acts. In these situations, an offering of such securities must comply with the registration and delivery requirements of the Securities Acts unless an exemption is available. The offering must also comply with the antifraud provisions of the Securities Acts and the supporting regulations.

Due to the complex nature of the securities laws, a developer should always seek the opinion of competent legal counsel in determining whether the sale of particular condominium units requires registration with the SEC or whether an exemption is available.

The following excerpt from SEC release 5347 is included solely for informative purposes:

> In summary, the offering of condominium units in conjunction with any one of the following will cause the offering to be viewed as an offering of securities in the form of investment contracts:
>
> 1. The condominiums, with any rental arrangement or other similar service, are offered and sold with emphasis on the economic benefits to the purchaser to be derived from the managerial efforts of the promoter, or a third party designated or arranged for by the promoter, from rental of the units;
>
> 2. The offering of participation in a rental pool arrangement; and
>
> 3. The offering of a rental or similar arrangement whereby the purchaser must hold his unit available for rental for any part of the year, must use an exclusive rental agent or is otherwise materially restricted in his occupancy or rental of his unit.
>
> In all of the above situations, investor protection requires the application of the federal securities laws.

Chapter 5

Criteria for Recording a Sale

In order to determine whether profit recognition is appropriate under the circumstances, the first test is to determine whether a sale should be recorded before going on to the next tests related to buyer's investment and seller's continuing involvement.

Timing of Recording a Sale

Generally, real estate sales should not be recorded prior to the time of closing. Since an exchange transaction is generally a prerequisite to recognizing profit, a sale must be consummated before recognizing profit on a sale of real estate. A sale is consummated when each of the following criteria is met:

- The parties are bound by the terms of a contract;
- All consideration has been exchanged; and
- All conditions precedent to closing have been performed.

Usually all of these conditions are met at the time of closing, not at the time of a contract to sell or a preclosing.

In addition, transactions should not be treated as sales for accounting purposes because of continuing seller's involvement, such as the following situations:

- The seller has an option or obligation to repurchase the property;
- The seller guarantees returns of the buyer's investment; or
- The seller retains an interest in the buyer as a general partner in a limited partnership and has a significant receivable.

Effect of Failure to Meet the Criteria for Recording a Sale. If the criteria for recording a sale are not met, the deposit, financing, lease, or profit sharing (co-venture) method should be used depending on the substance of the transaction.

Some of the more common problems with respect to recording a sale are summarized below.

Situations Which Do Not Meet the Criteria of Recording a Sale

Consideration Not Transferred. Frequently, a mortgage note is received as part of the consideration in a sale transaction. If, however, the mortgage note is not received by the seller, the date of the sale for accounting purposes must be delayed until the date the consideration is transferred.

Insignificant Down Payment. A transaction usually would not be recorded as a sale, for accounting purposes, when no down payment has been made by the buyer or when the down payment is so small that the substance of the transaction is an option arrangement. The deposit method described on page 132 would be appropriate in such cases.

Option or Obligation to Repurchase. A transaction is not a sale in substance if a seller has an obligation or an option to repurchase the property or a buyer has an option to compel the seller to repurchase. Paragraph 56 of the *Profit Recognition Accounting Guide* specifically provides that the existence of an option to repurchase prohibits sale recognition. (See page 77 for discussions of the accounting method to be followed in such instances.)

Anti-Speculation Clauses. Many developers include provisions in agreements to assure that the buyer adheres to the master development plan. Such provisions, frequently referred to as anti-speculation provisions, require the buyer to develop the land in a specified manner within a given period of time. The question often arises about how these anti-speculation provisions affect recording of a sale because they frequently represent options to repurchase which would prohibit sale recognition. For example, a sale agreement providing for a forced sale, in the event of a breach of an anti-speculation provision, is in substance a repurchase option if the seller either has the right to bid for the land or will sustain a portion of the loss on the sale. On the other hand, a sale agreement prohibiting disposition of the land without the prior written approval of the seller—in the event the buyer breaches his agreement to develop—is not by itself considered to be an impediment to recording a sale.

Guarantees of Return of Buyer Investment. Where the terms of the transaction are such that the buyer may expect to recover his investment plus a return through assured cash returns, subsidies, and net tax benefits—even if he were to default on his debt to the seller—the transaction is probably not in substance a sale. (See page 80 for discussion of the accounting method to be followed.)

Sales to Limited Partnerships. Where the seller is a general partner and has a significant receivable from the buyer, a sale cannot be recognized. A significant receivable is defined as 15 percent of the maximum first lien financing generally available. (See page 78 for discussion of the accounting method to be followed.)

Situations Which by Themselves Do Not Prohibit Recording a Sale

Transfer of Title Not Completed. When all other steps prerequisite to a sale have taken place, but the escrow agent or attorney does not record the transfer of title on a timely basis for reasons not significant to the transaction, the date of sale for accounting purposes would be the date the transfer of title could be recorded.

Closing Not Completed. Where a trustee is being used to handle the mechanics of the closing process and has possession of the title (and all other conditions have been met), but the actual closing has not taken place, the sale would not be delayed for accounting purposes even though the actual closing would not be carried out until a few days later. (If, however, the delay is due to contingencies which could prevent the ultimate closing, the sale cannot be recorded until the date that these contingencies are eliminated.)

Seller Has Right of First Refusal. Where the seller of a piece of property has the right of first refusal if the purchaser decides to sell the property, such a right is not considered to be an option. Thus, a seller would not be precluded from recording a sale.

Title Withheld as Security. Where title is withheld only as security for an unpaid receivable, the date of sale for accounting purposes would not be delayed if the sale would otherwise be recorded.

Development and Construction Not Complete. Exceptions to the "conditions precedent to closing" have been specifically provided where a sale of property includes a requirement for the seller to perform certain construction or development. The exceptions are permitted because of the length of the construction period and provide that under certain conditions, partial sale recognition is acceptable as construction progresses. This exception is not usually applicable to single family detached housing, which generally does not have a lengthy construction period. It should be pointed out that AICPA *Statement of Position 75–6* specifically resolved what appeared to be a conflict between paragraphs 47, 48, and 60 of the *Profit Recognition Accounting Guide,* which permits income recognition on a percentage of completion basis, and paragraph 14, which requires that all conditions precedent to closing must be performed.

Chapter 6

Tests for Profit Recognition – Adequacy of Down Payment

In order for the seller to record full profit recognition, the buyer's down payment must be adequate in size and in composition. Even if this test is met, still other tests must be met that relate to the receivable from the buyer and the seller's continued involvement.

SIZE OF DOWN PAYMENT

The minimum down payment requirement as set forth in paragraph 20 is one of the *Profit Recognition Accounting Guide*'s most important provisions. As a general rule, Exhibit A from the guide (see Table 6.1) sets forth minimum down payments ranging from 5 percent to 25 percent of sales value based upon usual loan limits for various types of properties. The minimum down payment percentages should be considered to be specific requirements.

If a newly placed permanent loan or firm permanent loan commitment for maximum financing exists, the minimum down payment must be the higher of (a) the amount derived from Exhibit A, or (b) the amount by which the sales value exceeds 115 percent of the new financing. An example illustrating this test is set forth in Table 6.2. Regardless of this test, in most instances a down payment of 25 percent of the property's sales value is usually sufficient to justify profit recognition at the time of sale. This percentage is deemed to represent a significant investment on the part of the buyer.

Table 6.1. Exhibit A—Minimum Down Payment Requirements

The following schedule of minimum down payments of various types of real estate property has been included in the Profit Recognition Accounting Guide to help determine whether a buyer's initial investment in the property is adequate to recognize profit at time of sale.

This schedule cannot cover every type of real estate property. To evaluate down payments on other types of property, analogies can be made to the types of properties specified, or the risks of a particular property can be related to the risks of the properties specified.

	Minimum down payment expressed as a percentage of sales value
Land:	
Held for commercial, industrial, or residential development to commence within two years after sale	20% (a)
Held for commercial, industrial, or residential development after two years	25% (a)
Commercial and industrial property:	
Office and industrial buildings, shopping centers, etc.:	
Properties subject to lease on a long-term lease basis to parties having satisfactory credit rating, cash flow currently sufficient to service all indebtedness	10%
Single tenancy properties sold to a user having a satisfactory credit rating	15%
All other	20%
Other income-producing properties (hotels, motels, marinas, mobile home parks, etc.):	
Cash flow currently sufficient to service all indebtedness	15%
Start-up situations or current deficiencies in cash flow	25%
Multi-family residential property:	
Primary residence:	
Cash flow currently sufficient to service all indebtedness	10%
Start-up situations or current deficiencies in cash flow	15%
Secondary or recreational residence:	
Cash flow currently sufficient to service all indebtedness	15%
Start-up situations or current deficiencies in cash flow	25%
Single family residential property (including condominium or co-operative housing):	
Primary residence of buyer	5% (b)
Secondary or recreational residence	10% (b)

(a) These percentages are not intended to apply to volume retail lot sales by land development companies where such sales are covered by the AICPA Accounting Guide entitled "Accounting for Retail Land Sales." Where such sales are not covered by this guide, the above percentages for land are applicable.

(b) As set forth in Exhibit A, "if collectibility of the remaining portion of the sales price cannot be supported by reliable evidence of collection experience, a higher down payment is indicated." When independent first mortgage financing is not utilized, the minimum down payment should not be less than 60% of the difference between the sales value and the financing available from loans guaranteed by regulatory bodies, such as FHA or VA, or from independent financial institutions. When independent first mortgage financing is utilized, the minimum down payment should not be less than the amount by which the sales value exceeds 115% of the new financing as set forth under the size test above.

Definition of Sales Value

The down payment requirements must be related to sales value, which is the stated sales price increased or decreased for such matters or other consideration that clearly constitute additional proceeds on the sale, services without adequate compensation and imputed interest. (See page 83 for discussion of services without adequate compensation and page 74 for discussion of imputed interest.) The stated sales price should represent the total consideration payable by the buyer. Therefore, the consideration payable for development work or improvements that are the responsibility of the seller should be included in the computation of sales value. An example illustrating the sales value versus the sales price is set forth in Table 6.3.

Leased Land

If improvements are sold subject to a lease of the underlying land from the seller/lessor to the buyer/lessee, to determine the adequacy of the down payment, the sales value should include the present value of the lease payments receivable computed at an appropriate interest or discount rate over the customary term of the indebtedness on the improvements. The interest or discount rate should be the rate for primary debt if the lease is not subordinated, or the rate for secondary debt if the lease is subordinated to loans with prior liens. (See pages 123 to 126 for profit recognition principles where a land lease in involved and Table 10.2 on page 125 for an example of the above principles to determine whether the down payment test has been met.)

COMPOSITION OF DOWN PAYMENT

It is important to determine what forms of consideration represent acceptable down payments. Cash payments from the buyer to the seller, of course, are usually the most common form. Other acceptable forms of down payment are:

- Buyer's notes, but only when supported by irrevocable letters of credit covering the period of the notes from an established lending institution which issues such letters in the normal course of business. As set forth in the AICPA *Statement of Position 75–6,* the down payment requirement is not met until the letters of credit are obtained;

- Cash payments by the buyer to third parties to reduce previously existing indebtedness; and
- Cash payments which are in substance additional sales proceeds, such as prepaid interest or fees that by the terms of the contract are maintained in an advance status and are applied against principal at a later date.

Some unacceptable forms of down payment are:

- Payments to third parties for improvements to the property;
- Prepaid interest payments which are not in substance additional sales proceeds;
- Marketable securities or other assets. The *Profit Recognition Accounting Guide* concluded in paragraph 22 that receipt of consideration constitutes down payment only at the time it is converted to cash;
- Buyer's notes without letters of credit—even when they are supported by the full faith and credit of the buyer;
- Funds received from the buyer from proceeds of priority loans on

Table 6.2. Down Payment Test—Exhibit A Versus New Financing

Assumptions	
Down payment paid to seller on sale of office building with adequate cash flow	$ 100,000
First mortgage (newly placed maximum financing with outside lender)	700,000
Second mortgage given to seller at market rate of interest	200,000
Sales value	$1,000,000
115% of first mortgage (1.15 × $700,000)	805,000
Down payment required under new financing test	$ 195,000

Result

Even if the down payment required under Exhibit A is only 10 percent ($100,000) the down payment is inadequate because the required test when there is a newly placed first mortgage is more restrictive requiring a down payment of $195,000.

Table 6.3.   Sales Value Versus Sales Price

Assumptions	
Down payment	$ 150,000
Balance of existing first mortgage payable by seller but assumed by buyer (market interest rate at time of sale is same as stated rate)	500,000
Second mortgage payable to seller—noninterest bearing	400,000
Stated sales price	$1,050,000
Amount required to discount second mortgage to fair market value ($400,000 less discounted value of $325,000)	75,000
Sales value	$ 975,000

Calculation of Down Payment
The down payment in relation to sales value is 15.5 percent. If it was computed in relation to sales price it is 14.3 percent. Thus, if the down payment required is 15 percent, this calculation demonstrates that the down payment test has been met.

the property. Under these circumstances, those funds have not come from the buyer and therefore do not provide assurance of collectibility of the remaining receivable. Those amounts should be excluded in determining the adequacy of the down payment; and

- Funds that have been or will be loaned to the buyer-builder/developer for acquisition, construction, or development purposes or otherwise provided directly or indirectly by the seller (including loan guarantees, collateral provided by the seller, and any other situation where the seller is subject to loss as a result of funds loaned to the buyer) must first be deducted from the down payment in determining whether the down payment test has been met.

The last point was clarified in AICPA *Statement of Position 75–6,* as follows:

Paragraph 22 does not require that the funds loaned by the seller be specifically identified with the funds comprising the down payment. As an example, if "A" sells unimproved land to "B" for $100,000, receives a down payment of $50,000 in cash, and plans to loan "B" $35,000 at some future date for installation of water and sewer lines, the down payment test has not been met. ($50,000 − $35,000 = $15,000 ÷ $100,000 = 15%; fails test as at least 20% is required.)

EFFECT OF INADEQUATE DOWN PAYMENT

If the buyer's down payment is inadequate, the accrual method of accounting is not appropriate and the deposit, installment or cost recovery method of accounting should be used. (See Chapter 11 for discussion and examples of when and how to use each of these methods.)

In the circumstances where the only other consideration besides cash that is received by the seller is the buyer's assumption of existing nonrecourse indebtedness, a sale could be recorded and profit recognized if all other conditions for recognizing a sale were met. However, if the buyer assumes recourse debt and the seller remains liable for the debt, he has a risk of loss comparable to the risk involved in holding a receivable from the buyer and therefore the accrual method would not be appropriate if the buyer's cash down payment is inadequate.

Chapter 7

Tests for Profit Recognition — Receivable from the Buyer

Even if the required down payment is made, a number of factors must be considered by the seller in connection with a receivable from the buyer. They include:

- Collectibility of receivable (see below).
- Buyer's continuing investment—amortization of receivable (see page 67).
- Future subordination (see page 70).
- Release provisions (see page 72).
- Imputation of interest (see page 74).

In addition, if the seller has any involvement with the buyer or the property other than collection of the receivable, further tests in connection with this involvement must be considered (see page 76). On a general note, the *Profit Recognition Accounting Guide,* in paragraph 15, indicates that:

> . . . a receivable supported by the full faith and credit of the buyer . . . is to be considered . . . to be the same as a receivable in which the seller has right of recourse only to the property sold.

ASSESSMENT OF COLLECTIBILITY OF RECEIVABLE

Collectibility of the receivable must be reasonably assured. It should be assessed in light of factors such as the credit standing of the buyer, cash flow from the property and the property's size and geographical location. This may be particularly important when the receivable is relatively short term and collectibility is questionable if the buyer will be required to obtain financing. In addition, a basic principle of real estate sales on credit is that the receivable must be adequately secured by the property sold. The thrust of the *Profit Recognition Accounting Guide* indicates that collectibility is not reasonably assured if the seller takes an unsecured note from the buyer.

BUYER'S CONTINUING INVESTMENT REQUIREMENT

The *Profit Recognition Accounting Guide* in paragraph 25 includes continuing investment requirements that must be met by the buyer (in addition to the down payment requirement) if the transaction is to be accounted for under the accrual method.

Tests for Full Profit Recognition

For full profit recognition, the buyer, as a minimum, must reduce his total indebtedness on the purchase price:

- Annually (beginning no more than one year after recording the sale);
- In level payments (including principal and interest); or
- Based upon amortization of the full amount over a maximum term of 20 years for land or the customary term of a first mortgage by an independent lender for other property.

Annual payments, in order to be acceptable, must begin within one year of recording the sale and meet the same composition test that is used in determining adequacy of down payments (see page 61). In determining the customary term of a first mortgage loan, the term of a new loan from an independent financial lending institution is usually considered to be the customary term. If there is an existing first mortgage lien placed in recent years, this term would normally be the term an independent financial institution would be willing to place on the property.

All indebtedness on the property need not be reduced proportionately. However, if the seller's receivable is not being amortized, realization may be in question and the collectibility must be more carefully assessed. Lump sum (balloon) payments do not affect the amortization requirement as long as the scheduled amortization is within the maximum period and the minimum annual amortization tests are met. For example, if the customary term of the mortgage by an independent lender required amortizing payments over 25 years, then the continuing investment requirement would be based on such an amortization schedule. If the terms of the receivable required principal and interest payments on such a schedule only for the first five years, with a balloon at the end of year five, the continuing investment requirements are met. In these cases, however, the collectibility of the balloon payment should be carefully assessed. An example illustrating full profit recognition is set forth in Table 7.1.

It should also be pointed out that imputation of management fees should be considered in the tests related to the buyer's continuing investment. As described on page 83, the sales price is reduced for services to be performed by the seller without adequate compensation in calculating sales value. This calculation is used for the test related to the adequacy of the down payment. It also is to be used in the tests related to the buyer's continuing investment. For example, in a situation where the seller is perform-

Table 7.1. Test for Full Profit Recognition Met

Assumptions	
Cash down payment	$ 50,000
Notes received from buyer supported by irrevocable letter of credit from an established lending institution	200,000
Total cash and cash equivalents	$ 250,000
First mortgage note from independent lender at market rate of interest (20 year term—meets required amortization)	550,000
Second mortgage note payable to seller, 12% (market rate) with quarterly payment of $7000 including interest	200,000
Total sales price and sales value	$1,000,000

Result

This sale meets the down payment test since the buyer's notes are acceptable as cash under the *Profit Recognition Accounting Guide*. The continuing investment requirements are also met, since the first mortgage note is amortizing and meets the maximum term test and the second mortgage will be amortized in 17 years, which is less than the customary term for a first mortgage loan. Accordingly, full profit recognition is appropriate.

ing management services for the buyer for two years without compensation, imputed management fees should first be deducted from any initial down payment received in excess of the minimum required. To the extent that imputed management fees cannot be applied to the excess of the minimum down payment required, such fees should next be deducted from subsequent payments received by the seller in determining that the buyer's continuing investment test has been met. (See page 83 for discussion of services without adequate compensation.)

Tests for Reduced Profit Recognition

If the amortization requirements as described above for full profit recognition are not met, a reduced profit may be recognized if the annual payments are at least equal to the sum of:

- Level annual payments of principal and interest on a maximum available first mortgage; and
- Interest at an appropriate rate on the remaining indebtedness payable by the buyer.

The reduced profit is calculated by valuing the receivable from the buyer at the present value of the lowest level of annual payments due over the customary term of the first mortgage. An example illustrating the calculation of reduced profit is set forth in Table 7.2.

CUMULATIVE APPLICATION OF CONTINUING INVESTMENT TESTS

The requirements for continuing investment previously described are cumulative and must be applied at the closing date and annually thereafter. Any excess of down payment received over the minimum required may be applied toward the continuing investment requirements. An example illustrating the cumulative application of excess down payment is set forth in Table 7.3.

The closing date for this purpose is the date of recording the sale for accounting purposes. Thus, in a change from the installment method to the accrual method, the closing date for this purpose is the date the transaction

Table 7.2.   Calculation of Reduced Profit

Assumptions		
Down payment (meets applicable tests)		$ 150,000
First mortgage note from independent lender at market rate of interest (new, 20 years—meets required amortization)		750,000
Second mortgage note payable to seller, interest at a market rate is due annually, with principal due at the end of the 25th year (the term exceeds the maximum permitted)		100,000
Stated selling price		$1,000,000
Adjustment Required in Valuation of		
Receivable From Buyer		
Second mortgage payable to seller	$100,000	
Less: present value of 20 years annual interest payments on second mortgage (lowest level of annual payments over customary term of first mortgage— thus, 20 years not 25)	70,000	30,000
Adjusted sales value for profit recognition		$ 970,000

The sales value as well as profit is reduced by $30,000. In some situations profit will be entirely eliminated by this calculation.

---

is originally recorded as an installment sale. An example illustrating the cumulative application of excess annual principal payments is set forth in Table 7.4.

If, however, the transaction was originally accounted for under the deposit method, the cumulative test would not apply until the sale is recorded for accounting purposes. In addition, the interest portion of the cash received under the deposit method can be included when determining the adequacy of the buyer's investment on a cumulative basis. In this case, however, the interest must also be included in sales value.

RECEIVABLE SUBJECT TO FUTURE SUBORDINATION

Land developers frequently sell land and receive, as part of the consideration, a receivable that can be subordinated to a future loan. For example, a developer sells lots to a builder and agrees that the receivable can be

Table 7.3.   Cumulative Application—Excess Down Payment

	Balloon payment due at end of	
	Fifth year	Sixth year
Assumptions		
Down payment on land to be developed within 2 years (20% required for full profit recognition)		$ 250,000
Mortgage given to seller at market rate of interest (10%) 25-year level payments with balloon payments as noted below		800,000
Sales value		$1,050,000
Cumulative principal amortization:		
20 year term (required for full profit recognition)	$ 85,275	$107,770
25 year term (actual term)	49,662	62,763
Continuing investment shortfall on cumulative basis	$ 35,613	$ 45,007
Cash down payment	$250,000	$250,000
Cash down payment required (20%)	210,000	210,000
Excess	40,000	40,000
Continuing investment shortfall	35,613	45,007
Excess (deficiency) of cumulative buyer investment	$ 4,387	($ 5,007)

Result

If the transaction requires the balloon payment at the end of the fifth year, full profit recognition is appropriate if the collectibility of the receivable is reasonably assured. If the transaction requires the balloon payment at the end of the sixth year, full profit recognition is not appropriate; the transaction should be accounted for under the installment method.

subordinated to a construction loan so that the builder can begin construction without paying off the debt issued with the land purchase.

When a receivable is subject to future subordination, profit recognition is limited to that which is calculated on the cost recovery method—unless the proceeds of the loan to which the receivable is subordinate are first to be used to reduce the seller's receivable. Although this accounting treatment is controversial, the cost recovery method is required under para-

Table 7.4.   Cumulative Application—Inadequate Down Payment but Excess Annual Principal Payments

---

Assumptions

Down payment on land to be developed within 2 years (inadequate because 20% is required for full profit recognition) $ 180,000

Mortgage given to seller at market rate of interest—10 year level amortization of principal plus interest payments   820,000

Sales value $1,000,000

Result

At closing, a sale may be recorded using the installment method. Since principal payments of $82,000 on the mortgage at the end of the first year would include excess cash of $42,000 based on a 20 year amortization of a receivable of $800,000, the 20 percent down payment test would be met at that time on a cumulative basis. This would allow the seller to switch from the installment method to the accrual method with full profit recognition.

---

graph 28 of the *Profit Recognition Accounting Guide* on the basis that collectibility of the sales price would not be reasonably assured. That is because the future subordination would permit the primary lender to obtain a prior lien on the property (leaving only a secondary residual value for the seller) and that the future loans could indirectly finance the buyer's initial cash investment. Future loans would include funds that the buyer receives from a permanent loan commitment existing at the time of the transaction.

The cost recovery method is not required if the receivable is subordinate to a mortgage currently existing on the property at the time of sale.

RELEASE PROVISIONS

If the sales transaction provides that part of a property may be released from liens securing related debt, the buyer must make adequate cumulative payments at the time of each release in relation to the sales value of the property not released in order for full profit recognition to be acceptable. The seller must look forward to each release date to determine if the investment test will be met at that time. An example illustrating release provisions is set forth in Table 7.5.

Table 7.5. Example of Release Provisions

Assumptions
1. Property sold—200 acres.
2. Value per acre—$5000.
3. All acres of equal value.
4. Development to commence immediately—
   therefore 20% down payment normally required.
5. Release requirements are:
   (a) 125% of selling price per acre.
   (b) All payments applied to release.
6. Composition of sales price

Down payment (25%)	$ 250,000
Mortgage to seller (10 years at 11%)	750,000
Sales price	$1,000,000

7. First release—55 acres at end of year one.

Analysis

Sales price $275,000 ($5000 × 55) × 125% = $343,750 required for release, paid as follows:

Down payment		$250,000
First installment of principal		44,850
Additional release payment (minimum required under agreement) to bring total payments to $343,750		48,900
		$343,750
Remaining unpaid balance ($1,000,000 less $343,750)		$656,250
Calculation with respect to remaining unreleased acres—145 acres × $5000 each (sales value)		$725,000
Down payment required (20% of $725,000)	$145,000	
Amount required for amortization of principal from date of sale to date of release equals $725,000 − $145,000 × 1.56% (1.56% is first year amortization of principal based upon a maximum allowed 20 year amortization)	9,048	154,048
Maximum allowed unpaid		$570,852

Result

Since the unpaid debt after the first release ($656,250) exceeds the maximum allowed to be unpaid ($570,852), full profit recognition is not appropriate. The 55 acres released can be accounted for as a separate sale and, therefore, full profit recognition would be appropriate at the time of sale. Although full profit on the unreleased acreage is not appropriate, a portion of the profit may be recognized under the installment method.

IMPUTATION OF INTEREST

As previously mentioned, sales value must be reduced for imputation of interest. Careful attention should therefore be given to the need for imputing interest under AICPA *Accounting Principles Board Opinion No. 21,* "Interest on Receivables and Payables." The Opinion could have a significant effect on the amount of profit or loss recognition. As stated in the first paragraph of the Opinion:

> The use of an interest rate that varies from prevailing interest rates warrants evaluation of whether the face amount and the stated interest rate of a note or obligation provide reliable evidence for properly recording the exchange and subsequent related interest.

If imputation of interest is necessary, the mortgage note receivable should be adjusted to its present value by discounting all future payments on the notes. This would be done by using an imputed rate of interest at the prevailing rates available for similar financing with independent financial institutions. A distinction must be made between first and second mortgage loans because the appropriate imputed rate for a second mortgage is normally significantly higher than the rate for a first mortgage loan. It may be necessary to obtain independent valuations to assist in the determination of the proper rate.

Paragraph 13 of APB 21 gives some guidelines for determining an appropriate rate:

> The variety of transactions encountered precludes any specific interest rate from being applicable in all circumstances. However, some general guides may be stated. The choice of a rate may be affected by the credit standing of the issuer, restrictive covenants, the collateral, payment, and other terms pertaining to the debt, and, if appropriate, the tax consequences to the buyer and seller. The prevailing rates for similar instruments of issuers with similar credit ratings will normally help determine the appropriate interest rate for determining the present value of a specific note at its date of issuance. In any event, the rate used for valuation purposes will normally be at least equal to the rate at which the debtor can obtain financing of a similar nature from other sources at the date of the transaction. The objective is to approximate the rate which would have resulted if an independent borrower and an independent lender had negotiated a similar transaction under comparable terms and conditions

with the option to pay the cash price upon purchase or to give a note for the amount of the purchase which bears the prevailing rate of interest to maturity.

An example illustrating imputation of interest on a second mortgage is set forth in Table 7.6.

Table 7.6. Imputation of Interest on a Second Mortgage

Assumptions	
Down payment	$ 200,000
First mortgage (newly placed with outside lender) bearing interest at 9½%	700,000
Second mortgage given to seller, requiring annual payments of $27,174 for 10 years, including interest at 6% (market rate for this type of loan is 12%)	200,000
Sale price	$1,100,000

Accounting Required by the Seller

The second mortgage would have to be recorded at $153,539 (present value of annuity of $27,174 for 10 years yielding 12 percent) with a corresponding reduction of sales value to $1,053,539. The seller would record interest income based upon an annual rate of 12 percent of the carrying value. The difference between this amount and the annual payment of $27,174 would be reflected as a reduction of the net carrying value of the second mortgage receivable.

Amortization of Discount. The discount resulting from imputation of interest should be accounted for as an element of interest over the life of the note using the "interest method," that is, amortizing the discount in such a way as to produce a constant rate of interest income when applied to the carrying value during any given period.

EFFECT OF FAILING TESTS RELATED
TO RECEIVABLES

If the criteria for recording a sale have been met but the tests related to the collectibility of the receivable as described here are not met, the accrual method of accounting is not appropriate and the installment or cost recovery method of accounting should be used. (See pages 136 to 142 for discussion and examples of when and how to use each of these methods.)

Chapter 8

Tests for Profit Recognition –
Seller's Continued Involvement

A seller sometimes continues to be involved over extended periods with property he has legally sold. This involvement may take many forms, such as:

Financing	Repurchasing
Management	Guarantees
Development	Equity participation
Construction	Leasebacks

When a seller has continued involvement, with respect to profit recognition, two general principles should be addressed:

- A sales contract should not be accounted for as a sale if the seller's continued involvement with the property carries in essence the same kinds of risks as does ownership of property; and
- Profit recognition should follow performance and in some cases should be postponed completely until a later date.

The application of these general principles is discussed in the following sections as they relate to the various common types of continuing involvement summarized as follows:

Seller involvement not requiring deferral of sale or profit recognition:

- Participation solely in future profit (see page 77).

Seller involvement requiring deferral of recording of the sale:

- Option or obligation to repurchase the property, including buyer's option to compel seller to repurchase (see below);
- General partner in a limited partnership with a significant receivable from the partnership (see page 78);
- Responsibility for permanent financing (see page 80);
- Guaranteed return of buyer's investment (see page 80).

Seller involvement usually requiring deferral of all or a portion of profit:

- Guaranteed returns to buyer including sale-leaseback (see page 81);
- Services without adequate compensation (see page 83);
- Development and construction (see page 83);
- Initiation and support of operations (see page 86);
- Partial sales—sale of partial interest or sale to the buyer in which the seller has an equity interest (see page 89).

PARTICIPATION SOLELY IN FUTURE PROFITS

Sales of real estate may include or be accompanied by an agreement that provides for the seller to participate in future operating profits or residual values. As long as the seller has no further obligations or risk of loss, profit recognition on the sale need not be deferred. A receivable from the buyer is permitted if the other provisions for profit recognition are met, but no costs can be deferred. These costs would include investment costs remaining on the seller's books.

OPTION OR OBLIGATION TO REPURCHASE THE PROPERTY

As set forth in paragraph 56 of the *Profit Recognition Accounting Guide,* when the seller has the option or obligation to repurchase property (including the buyer's option to compel the seller to repurchase), a sale cannot be recognized. However, neither a commitment by the seller to assist or use his best efforts (with appropriate compensation) on a resale, nor a right of first refusal based on a bona fide offer by a third party, would preclude sale recognition. The accounting to be followed would depend on the repurchase terms.

Obligation to Repurchase at a Higher Price. When the seller has an obligation to repurchase the property at a price higher than the total amount of the payments received and to be received, the transaction is a financing arrangement. The arrangement should be accounted for under the financing method requiring accrual of interest expense. (See page 142.)

Option to Repurchase at a Higher Price. In the case of a repurchase option at a higher price, if the surrounding facts and circumstances at the time of the sale transaction indicate a presumption or a likelihood that the seller will exercise his option, the financing method described on page 142. should be used as if there is an obligation to repurchase. Examples of surrounding facts and circumstances may include revised value of property, integral part of development and management intention. If such a presumption does not exist at the time of the sale transaction, the deposit method as set forth on page 132 is appropriate.

Obligation or Option to Repurchase at a Lower Price. In the case of a repurchase obligation or option at a lower price, the transaction usually is in substance a lease or is part lease/part financing and should be accounted for under the lease method as described on page 142.

Option to Repurchase at an Undetermined Market Price. In the case of an option to repurchase at a market price to be determined in the future, the transaction should be accounted for under the deposit method as set forth on page 132.

GENERAL PARTNER IN A LIMITED PARTNERSHIP WITH A SIGNIFICANT RECEIVABLE

When the seller is a general partner, in a limited partnership, and has a significant receivable (in excess of 15 percent of available first lien financing) related to the property, the transaction would not qualify as a sale. Such a transaction should usually be accounted for as a profit sharing arrangement as discussed on page 143. Accounting for such a transaction as a profit sharing (or co-venture) arrangement is necessary to properly reflect the substance of the transaction. It should be used to adequately reflect that all of the risks and rewards of ownership have not been transferred.

Paragraph 53 of the *Profit Recognition Accounting Guide* is quite specific in defining a significant receivable as a:

> receivable in excess of 15% of the maximum first lien financing that could be obtained from an established lending institution for the property sold and would include the following:
>
> 1. A construction loan made or to be made by the seller to the extent that it exceeds the minimum funding commitment for permanent financing from a third party on which the seller will have no personal liability.
> 2. An all-inclusive or wrap around receivable held by the seller to the extent that it exceeds prior lien financing for which the seller has no personal liability.
> 3. Other funds provided or to be provided directly or indirectly (including liability on indebtedness) by the seller to the buyer or holder of the property, and
> 4. The present value of a land lease when the seller is the lessor.

An example illustrating the calculation of a significant receivable is set forth in Table 8.1.

Table 8.1.   Calculation of Significant Receivable

Assume the sale of a property under the following terms to a limited partnership in which the seller is a general partner:	
Down payment paid to seller	$ 300,000
First mortgage assumed by buyer/limited partnership (newly placed with outside lender—maximum financing available)	750,000
Second mortgage given to seller/general partner by buyer at market rate of interest	150,000
Sales value	$1,200,000
15% of the available first lien financing (15% of $750,000)	$ 112,500

The receivable amounting to $150,000 held by the seller/general partner exceeds 15 percent of the available first lien financing and therefore would be considered a significant receivable. Under this situation, the transaction would not qualify as a sale even though the down payment may have been adequate.

RESPONSIBLE FOR PERMANENT FINANCING

When the seller is responsible for obtaining or providing permanent financing for the buyer, obtaining the financing is a prerequisite to accounting for the transaction as a sale. It should be noted, however, that even if obtaining financing is not the obligation of the seller, in many cases, collectibility of the receivable may be questionable and the obligation of the seller might be presumed if the buyer does not have financing. As described on page 66, collectibility of the receivable must be reasonably assured.

If sale recognition is not appropriate, the deposit method described on page 132 is appropriate if the lack of financing is the only impediment to recording a sale.

GUARANTEED RETURNS TO BUYER

In some cases, the seller will guarantee certain returns to the buyer. This usually will limit profit recognition and may prohibit the recognition of a sale. Guarantees are discussed below according to their nature.

Guaranteed Return of Buyer's Investment

Paragraph 13 of the *Profit Recognition Accounting Guide* indicates that if:

> the terms of a transaction are such that the buyer may expect to recover his investment plus a return through assured cash returns, subsidies, and net tax benefits, even if he were to default on his debt to the seller the transaction is probably not in substance a sale. . . .

Such a transaction should not be accounted for as a sale but usually should be accounted for as a profit sharing agreement as described on page 143.

In the case of transactions involving assured cash returns and subsidies, it should be readily ascertainable if the buyer can expect to recover his investment plus a return. It becomes more complicated, however, if the seller must calculate the buyer's net tax benefits to combine such benefits with the guaranteed payments.

The 1976 revisions to the Internal Revenue Code regarding construction period interest and taxes, depreciation recapture, prepaid interest, and guaranteed payments have reduced the opportunities where (at the time of the transaction) the buyer may expect net tax benefits after giving consideration to recapture provisions. Opportunities still exist for sale of low-income housing, however, where the rules for depreciation recapture and construction period interest are not as stringent. Regardless, before a sale may be recorded, the computation of net tax benefits may be required in some circumstances to determine that this test has been met.

Sale-Leaseback

A guarantee of cash flow to the buyer sometimes takes the form of a leaseback arrangement. Since the earnings process in this situation has not usually been completed, profits on the sale should be deferred and amortized. On the other hand, losses on the sale will usually have been determined and therefore should be recognized immediately. The Financial Accounting Standards Board has issued *Statements of Financial Accounting Standards No. 13,* "Accounting for Leases" and *No. 28,* "Accounting for Sales with Leasebacks," that establish standards of accounting for such transactions.

Profit Recognition.   Profits should be deferred and amortized in a manner consistent with the classification of the leaseback:

- If the leaseback is an operating lease, deferred profit should be amortized in proportion to the related gross rental charged to expense over the lease term; or
- If the leaseback is a capital lease, deferred profit should be amortized in proportion to the amortization of the leased asset. Effectively, the sale is treated as a financing transaction and the deferred profit should be offset in the balance sheet against the capitalized asset.

In situations where the leaseback covers only a minor portion of the property sold, or the period is relatively minor compared to the remaining useful life of the property, it may be appropriate to recognize all or a portion of the gain as income. Sales with minor leasebacks should be accounted for based on the separate terms of the sale and the leaseback unless the rentals called for by the leaseback are unreasonable in relation to current market conditions. If rentals are considered to be unreasonable, they must be adjusted to a reasonable amount in computing the profit on the sale.

The leaseback is considered to be minor when the present value of the leaseback based on reasonable rentals is 10 percent or less of the fair value of the asset sold. If the leaseback is not considered to be minor, but less than substantially all of the use of the asset is retained through a leaseback, profit may be recognized to the extent it exceeds the present value of the minimum lease payments in the case of an operating lease or the recorded amount of the leased asset in the case of a capital lease.

Loss Recognition.   Losses should be recognized immediately to the extent that the undepreciated cost (net carrying value) exceeds the fair value of the property. Fair value is frequently determined by the selling price from which the loss on the sale is measured. Many sale-leasebacks, however, are entered into as a means of financing, or for tax reasons, or both. The terms of the leaseback are negotiated as a package. Because of the interdependence of the sale and concurrent leaseback, the selling price in some cases is not representative of fair value. It would not be appropriate to recognize a loss on the sale that would be offset by future profits as a result of either reduced rental costs under an operating lease or depreciation and interest charges under a capital lease. Therefore, to the extent that the fair value is greater than the sale price, losses should be deferred and amortized in the same manner as profits.

Guarantee of Cash Flow Other than Sale-Leaseback

A guarantee by the seller of cash flow to the buyer on the sale of an operating property is discussed on page 87.

When the seller guarantees cash returns to the buyer on the sale of a nonoperating property, the accounting method to be followed depends upon whether or not the seller's expected cost of the guarantee is determinable.

Guarantee Amount Determinable.   If the amount can be reasonably estimated, the seller should record the guarantee as a cost at the time of sale, thus either reducing the profit or increasing the loss on the transaction.

Guarantee Amount Not Determinable. If the amount cannot be reasonably estimated, the transaction is probably in substance a profit sharing or co-venture arrangement. See page 143 for a discussion of this method of accounting.

Guarantee Amount Not Determinable But Is Limited. If the amount cannot be reasonably estimated but a maximum cost of the guarantee is determinable, the seller may record the maximum cost of the guarantee as a cost at the time of sale, thus either reducing the profit or increasing the loss on the transaction. Alternatively, the seller may account for the transaction as described in the preceding paragraph as if the guarantee amount is not determinable.

SERVICES WITHOUT ADEQUATE COMPENSATION

When a sales contract is accompanied by an agreement to provide management services without adequate compensation, the value of the services should be imputed, deducted from the sales price and recognized over the term of the management contract.

For example, the seller of an apartment complex may agree as part of the sale transaction to continue managing the complex for the next two years. In determining the sales value, the management contract should be valued at the amount the seller would charge an independent party for this service. That amount should be deducted from the selling price and amortized into income over the two year contract period. An example illustrating the adjustment required is set forth in Table 8.2.

This does not imply that profit recognition at the time of any sale is appropriate as long as future costs and the value of services to be rendered can be estimated. This is not always the case when the management contract cannot be cancelled and the compensation is unusual for the services to be rendered. This situation is described in the section discussing implied support of operations on page 87.

DEVELOPMENT AND CONSTRUCTION

A sale of undeveloped or partially developed land may include or be accompanied by an agreement requiring future seller performance for devel-

Table 8.2.   Services Without Adequate Compensation

Assumptions	
1. Stated sales transaction for sale of an apartment:	
Down payment	$300,000
Balance of existing first mortgage from independent lender	
at market rate	400,000
Second mortgage payable to seller at market rate	100,000
Stated sales price	$800,000
2. Cost of apartment	$550,000

3. Seller is to provide management services for two years without compensation.
4. Similar management services in the area can be obtained for $36,000 annually.
5. Tests relating to the buyer's continuing investment have been met and the down payment exceeds the minimum required by more than the normal management fee of $72,000.*

Calculation of Profit	
Sales price as above	$800,000
Less: imputed amount required to compensate seller for management of the complex for the next two years	72,000
Sales value	$728,000
Less: cost of apartment	550,000
Total profit	$178,000

Assuming all other profit recognition tests are met, the profit of $178,000 would be recognized at closing. The seller's compensation for management services is amortized to revenue at the rate of $3,000 each month over the two year period in order to match the expenses incurred in management and earn a normal profit thereon.

Note. In this illustration, the excess down payment is sufficient to cover the management fees. If the down payment was only sufficient to meet the minimum required, the imputed management fees would have to be deducted from other receivables from the buyer, using present value techniques. In some situations, this could cause the seller to fail tests relating to the buyer's continuing investment.

as costs associated with syndication or other fees earned by the seller. The buyer's initial and continuing investment tests, of course, must be met as related to the total sales value. An example illustrating the cost incurred method is set forth in Table 8.3.

Table 8.3.   Cost Incurred Method

Assumptions
1. Sale of land for commercial development—$475,000.
2. Development contract—$525,000.
3. Down payment and other buyer investment requirements met.
4. Land cost—$200,000.
5. Development costs—$500,000 (reliably estimated)—$325,000 incurred in initial year.

Calculation of Profit to be Recognized in Initial Year

Sale of land	$ 475,000
Development contract price	525,000
Total sales price	1,000,000
Costs:	
Land	200,000
Development	500,000
Total costs	700,000
Total profit anticipated	$ 300,000
Cost incurred through end of initial year:	
Land	$ 200,000
Development	325,000
Total	$ 525,000
Profit to be recognized in initial year—$525,000 ÷ $700,000 × 300,000 =	$ 225,000

INITIATION AND SUPPORT OF OPERATIONS

If the property sold is an operating property (for example, an apartment house, a shopping center, an office building, or a warehouse) as opposed to a nonoperating property (for example, a land lot, a condominium unit, or single family detached housing), deferral of all or a portion of the profit

opment or construction. Deferral of all or a portion of the profit is app
priate in these circumstances. If the property that is sold and being
veloped is an operating property—such as an apartment, a shopping cen
or an office building—as opposed to a nonoperating property—such a
land lot, a condominium unit, or single family detached housing—the s
tion on initiation and support of operations on page 86 may also apply.

If there is a time lapse between the sale agreement and the future p
formance agreement, deferral provisions would usually apply if definit
development plans existed at the time of sale and the parties anticipate
development contract when they entered into the sales contract. In ad
tion paragraph 50 of the *Profit Recognition Accounting Guide* states:

> A seller's continuing involvement for future development or construc-
> tion work may be presumed if a buyer is financially unable to pay
> amounts due for development or construction work or has the right under
> the terms of the arrangement to defer payment until the work is done.

Completed Contract Method

If a seller is obligated to develop the property or construct facilities an
total costs and profit cannot be reliably estimated, profit should be de
ferred until the contract is completed or until such time as the total cost
and profit can be reliably estimated. For example, total costs and profit
may not be reliably estimated when the development is deferred, the selle
lacks experience, or the development plans are not sufficiently defined.

Under the completed contract method, all profit, including profit on the
sale of land, would be deferred until the seller's obligations were fulfilled.

Cost Incurred Method

If costs and profit can be reliably estimated, profit recognition over the
improvement period is required on the basis of costs incurred (including
land) as a percentage of total costs to be incurred. Thus, if the land was
a principal part of the sale and its market value greatly exceeded cost, part
of the profit that could be said to be related to the land sale would be deferred and recognized during the development or construction period. The
same rate of profit must be used for all seller costs connected with the
transaction. For this purpose the cost of development work or improvements that are the responsibility of the seller should be included, as well

may be required under paragraphs 51–55 of the *Profit Recognition Accounting Guide* that establishes guidelines for not only stated support but also for implied support. Although those provisions would not ordinarily apply to undeveloped or partially developed land, if the buyer has commitments to construct operating properties, these guidelines should apply if there is stated or implied support. Assuming the criteria for recording a sale and the tests of buyer's investment are met, the following sets forth guidelines for profit recognition where there is stated or implied support.

Stated Support

Guaranteed Returns to the Buyer. When the seller contractually guarantees cash returns on investments to the buyer, profit recognition should not begin until such time as actual rental operations are at a level sufficient to cover all obligations, such as operating expenses, debt service, and other contractual payments, including payments to the seller.

Other Guaranteed Support. Other guaranteed support is treated differently from guaranteed returns to the buyer. If, for example, the seller guaranteed the buyer that there would be no negative cash flow from the project, but did not guarantee a positive return on investment, then profit recognition spread over the support period, as described here, should begin earlier. Of course, there must be objective information regarding occupancy levels and rental rates in the immediate area, to provide reasonable assurance that rental income will be sufficient to meet those expenses and cash flow requirements.

Implied Support

The seller is presumed to be obligated to initiate and support operations of property he has sold, even in the absence of specified requirements in the sale contract or related document. The conditions under which support is implied are described in paragraph 52 of the *Profit Recognition Accounting Guide:*

> A seller obtains an interest as general partner in a limited partnership that acquires an interest in the property sold.
> A seller retains an equity interest in the property, such as an undivided

interest or an equity interest in a joint venture that holds an interest in the property.

A seller holds a receivable from a buyer for a significant part of the sales price and collection of the receivable is dependent upon the operation of the property.

A seller enters into a management contract with the buyer that provides for compensation on terms not usual for the services to be rendered and that is not terminable by either seller or buyer.

It should be noted that when the seller is a general partner in a limited partnership and has a significant receivable related to the property, the transaction should not be accounted for as a sale (see page 78).

Where there is implied support, profit should be spread over the support period as described below.

Profit Recognition Where There Is Stated or Implied Support

When commencement of profit recognition is appropriate, the following general rules apply:

- Profit is recognized on the basis of costs incurred as compared to the total costs to be incurred. Costs include land and operating expenses during the rent-up period as well as other costs. Revenues for gross profit purposes would include rent from operations during the rent-up period.
- As set forth in paragraph 55 of the *Profit Recognition Accounting Guide:*

  . . . support should be presumed for at least two years from the time of initial rental unless actual rental operations are able earlier to cover all obligations, such as operating expenses, debt service, and other contractual commitments including payments to the seller.

Where the seller is contractually obligated for a longer period of time, profit recognition should be spread over the contractual period.

Estimated rental income should be adjusted by reducing estimated future rent receipts by a safety factor of 33⅓% unless signed lease agreements have been obtained to support a projection higher than the rental level thus computed. As set forth in AICPA *Statement of Position 75–6,* when signed leases amount to more than 66⅔% of estimated rents, no additional safety factor is required—but only amounts under signed lease agreements can be included. An example illustrating the calculation of safety factor is set forth in Table 8.4.

Table 8.4.   Calculation of Safety Factor

Assumptions
  1. *A* sells an office building under development to *B* together with an agreement to support operations for 3 years.
  2. Projected annual rent roll is $1,000,000 of which $350,000 is supported by signed lease agreements.
  3. Projected rental income for years 1 through 3 is $600,000, $750,000 and $1,000,000, respectively.

Calculation of Safety Factor
At the time of sale, the revenues to be included in the calculation would be computed as follows:

Year	Projected Rental Income	Safety Factor (33⅓%)	Adjusted Projected Rental Income
1	$ 600,000	$200,000	$400,000
2	750,000	250,000	500,000
3	1,000,000	333,333	666,667

If there were signed lease agreements in the amount of $500,000 at the time of sale, the amount used in year 1 would be $500,000 because it is greater than the adjusted projected rental income. The adjusted projected rental income would remain as computed for years 2 and 3.

PARTIAL SALES

A partial sale would include the following types of real estate sales:

* A sale of an interest in real estate;
* A sale of real estate where the seller has an equity interest in the buyer (for example, a joint venture, or a partnership); and/or
* A sale of a condominium unit. (See Chapter 9.)

Sale of an Interest in Property

Profit recognition is not precluded in a sale of a partial interest if all of the following conditions exist:

- Sale is to an independent buyer;
- Collection of sales price is reasonably assured;
- The seller is not required to support the property, its operations or related obligations to an extent greater than the seller's proportionate interest; and/or
- The buyer does not have preferences to profits or cash flow. (If the buyer has such preferences, the cost recovery method is required under paragraph 59 of the *Profit Recognition Accounting Guide*. See page 140 for application of the cost recovery method.)

In the case of a sale of a partial interest in operating properties, if the conditions described in the preceding paragraph are met, profit recognition must be spread as described on page 87, as there is an implied presumption that the seller is obligated to support the operations.

Seller Has Equity Interest in the Buyer

No profit may be recognized if the seller controls the buyer. If the seller does not control the buyer, profit recognition, to the extent of the other investors' proportionate interests, is appropriate if all other necessary requirements for profit recognition are satisfied. The portion of the profit applicable to the equity interest of the seller/investor should be deferred until such costs are charged to operations by the venture. Again, regarding a sale of operating properties, even the portion of the profit relating to other investor's interest must be spread, as described on page 87, because there is an implied presumption that the seller is obligated to support the operations. An example illustrating a sale to a joint venture in which the seller has an equity interest is set forth in Table 8.5.

Table 8.5. Sale to a Joint Venture in Which Seller Has an Equity Interest

---

Assumptions
1. Investor A sells land with an original cost of $60,000 to a 20 percent-owned joint venture (general partnership) for $100,000.
2. The venture is in the development stage and has no income or loss.
2. There is no other continuing involvement of Investor A requiring deferral of profit.

Accounting by the Seller/Investor
A's income for the year includes a gain on the sale as follows:

Selling price	$100,000
Cost of sales	60,000
Gross profit	40,000
Less: deferred profit of 20%	8,000
Gain on sale	$ 32,000

Since A's venture interest is 20%, A has made a sale to itself to that extent and a sale to its joint venture partners to the extent of 80%. Therefore, A should defer 20% of the profit on the $100,000 sale and recognize it when the land is sold to a third party. A must reduce its gain of $40,000 by $8,000 (20% $\times$ $40,000 = $8,000).

Chapter 9

Accounting for Condominium Sales

In recent years, condominium developments have represented a significant segment of new home sales. While the condominium form of ownership has been widely used for many years in Europe and South America, this form of ownership did not gain wide acceptance in the United States until the 1960s.

One of the more significant events in condominium history in the United States was the enactment of Section 234 of the National Housing Act in 1961. The principal purpose of the Act was to extend Federal Housing Authorities' insurance to mortgage loans issued to residents of Puerto Rico. Because of high population concentrations and the island's need for middle-income developments in urban centers at the time, it was hoped that lending institutions—which had previously balked at making condominium mortgage loans for such projects—might channel funds into this area under the federal insurance program.

While this Act has only been utilized in the United States to a limited degree, it was a declaration of confidence by Congress and the Federal Housing Authorities in the condominium form of ownership. It also is credited with providing the impetus for state legislatures to enact condominium legislation. Every state now has a condominium law.

In addition, there are many other regulations affecting condominium sales and ownership. Both the Interstate Land Sales Full Disclosure Act and regulations prescribed by the Securities and Exchange Commission affect accounting for condominium sales by stipulating situations when an apparent sale may be voidable at the purchaser's option. They also provide for registration and reporting requirements. (See Chapter 4 for additional information regarding these regulations.)

A condominium, normally, is described as a multi-unit structure in which persons hold fee simple title to individual units (apartments) together with an undivided interest in the common elements associated with the structure. The common elements comprise all portions of the property other than the individual units and may include such items as the hallways and elevators contained in the building, the underlying land, private roads, parking areas and recreation facilities.

The definition of a condominium, however, varies by state. In certain states, the units need not be part of a multi-unit structure, thereby making possible a condominium subdivision of single-family detached homes. In other states, units need not consist of enclosed space, thereby permitting condominium campsites. As a result, there is a wide variety of condominiums which vary in use such as a (a) *primary residence,* (b) *secondary residence,* often oriented toward recreational facilities, or (c) *commercial property.*

In many instances, the uses can be commingled as in a high-rise condominium where the lower floors may contain commercial units while the upper floors contain single family residences. Some of the various types of residential condominiums are as follows:

- High-rise condominiums—usually four floors or more with elevator service;
- Mid-rise or horizontal condominiums—usually two to four floors without elevator service;
- Garden condominiums—a multi-unit structure one unit high; however, the units may contain two or three floors;
- Townhouse condominiums—normally distributed in clusters with five or less units; and/or
- Detached single-family condominium homes.

In addition, the rights of ownership of condominium units may vary substantially. They may be:

- Standard—owner has fee simple title to the unit with no substantial restrictions on its use;
- Restricted—owner has fee simple title; however, he may only occupy the unit for a stated period of time each year. During the remaining period, the unit is held for rent to the public; and

- Timesharing—two or more owners hold individually undivided interests in a given unit. Through a separate agreement, each owner may only occupy the unit during stated period(s) each year.

There is, then, a wide variety of the form and use of condominiums. Since its introduction, the condominium form of ownership has created several unique problems for developers and their accountants.

CONDOMINIUM ASSOCIATION

Since the administration of a property is of paramount importance to all unit owners, a property owners' association is generally established, with each owner subscribing to membership in the association. The sole purpose of the association is to manage the common properties. Each unit owner pays the association his proportionate share of the cost of managing the properties, including the cost of maintenance, repair, replacement and operation. The association may be established as either a partnership or a not-for-profit corporation. The corporate form, however, is most prevalent. Accounting for condominium associations is not covered in this book but the Community Associations Institute and Urban Land Institute have published a booklet entitled *Financial Management of Condominium and Homeowners' Associations,* which is useful in this area.

ACCOUNTING BACKGROUND

Prior to 1973, there was virtually no authoritative literature on accounting for sales of condominiums because the condominium was still a relatively new form of ownership. The following are excerpts from some of the earlier and more significant AICPA pronouncements discussing overall concepts of revenue recognition, from which current accounting principles for condominium sales have been developed:

- *Accounting Research Bulletin No. 43,* Chapter 11—"Government Contracts, Section A—Cost-Plus-Fixed-Fee Contracts":

  Paragraph 11—It is recognized that income should be recorded and stated in accordance with certain accounting principles as to time and amount; that profit is deemed to be realized when a sale in the ordinary course of business is effected unless the circumstances are such that collection of the sales price is not reasonably assured; and that delivery of goods sold under contract is normally regarded as the test of realization of profit or loss.

Paragraph 12—In the case of manufacturing, construction, or service contracts, profits are not ordinarily recognized until the right to full payment has become unconditional, i.e., when the product has been delivered and accepted, when the facilities are completed and accepted, or when the services have been fully and satisfactorily rendered. This accounting procedure has stood the test of experience and should not be departed from except for cogent reasons.

Paragraph 13—It is, however, a generally accepted accounting procedure to accrue revenues under certain types of contracts and thereby recognize profits, on the basis of partial performance, where the circumstances are such that total profit can be estimated with reasonable accuracy and ultimate realization is reasonably assured. Particularly where the performance of a contract requires a substantial period of time from inception to completion, there is ample precedent for pro rata recognition of profit as the work progresses, if the total profit and the ratio of the performance to date to the complete performance can be computed reasonably and collection is reasonably assured. Depending upon the circumstances, such partial performance may be established by deliveries, expenditures, or percentage of completion otherwise determined. This rule is frequently applied to long-term construction and other similar contracts . . .

- *Accounting Research Bulletin No. 45,* "Long-Term Construction-Type Contracts":

Paragraph 3—Two accounting methods commonly followed by contractors are the percentage of completion method and the completed contract method.

Paragraph 15—The committee believes that in general when estimates of costs to complete and extent of progress toward completion of long-term contracts are reasonably dependable, percentage-of-completion method is preferable. When lack of dependable estimates or inherent hazards cause forecasts to be doubtful, the completed-contract method is preferable. Disclosure of the method followed should be made.

- *APB Statement No. 4,* "Basic Concepts and Accounting Principles Underlying Financial Statements of Business Enterprises":

Paragraph 150—Revenue is conventionally recognized at a specific point in the earning process of a business enterprise, usually when assets are sold or services are rendered. This conventional recognition is the basis

of the pervasive measurement principle known as realization . . .
Revenue is generally recognized when both of the following conditions
are met: (1) the earning process is complete or virtually complete, and
(2) an exchange has taken place.

Paragraph 152—Revenue is sometimes recognized on bases other
than the realization rule. For example, on long-term construction contracts revenue may be recognized as construction progresses. This exception to the realization principle is based on the availability of evidence of the ultimate proceeds and the consensus that a better measure
of periodic income results.

CRITERIA FOR PROFIT RECOGNITION

The *Profit Recognition Accounting Guide* sets forth various general principles of accounting for profit on sales of real estate, including condominiums. The following is a summary of the criteria, based on those general
principles, which must be met prior to recognition of any profit on the
sale of a dwelling unit in a condominium project.

Time of sale for accounting purposes criteria include:

- All parties must be bound by the terms of the contract (page 97);
- All conditions precedent to closing, except completion of the project,
  must be performed (page 98).

Buyer's investment in purchased property criteria include:

- An adequate cash down payment must be received by the seller (see
  page 99);
- The buyer must be required to adequately increase his investment in
  the property annually—this commitment must be adequately secured
  (see page 100).

Seller's continued involvement with property sold criteria include:

- The developer must not have an option or obligation to repurchase
  the property (see page 102).

Additional criteria that have been established specifically for use of the
percentage of completion method:

- The developer must have the ability to estimate costs not yet incurred (see page 103);
- Construction must be beyond a preliminary stage (see page 103);
- Sufficient units must be sold to assure that the property will not revert to rental property (see page 104); and/or
- The developer must be able to reasonably estimate aggregate sales proceeds (see page 104).

The remainder of this section will interpret these criteria.

TIME OF SALE

The *Profit Recognition Accounting Guide* sets forth the general rule regarding time of sale in paragraph 14:

> Since an exchange transaction is generally a prerequisite to recognizing profit, the Committee concludes that a sale must be consummated before recognizing profit on a sale of real estate . . . A sale is consummated when the parties are bound by the terms of a contract, all consideration has been exchanged, and all conditions precedent to closing have been performed. Usually all of those conditions are met at the time of closing, not at the time of a contract to sell or a preclosing.

All Parties Must Be Bound by the Terms of the Contract

In order for the buyer to be bound, he must be unable to require a refund. Some states require that a "Declaration of Condominium" be filed with the appropriate authorities before the sales contract is binding and not voidable at the option of the buyer. Local state law, therefore, must be reviewed to determine if there is such a requirement and, if so, whether the sales contract is binding on the buyer.

Sometimes sales contracts include a condition that the document is binding only if permanent financing at an acceptable cost is available to the buyer at the time of closing. Recognition of a sale should be deferred until this condition is met.

In addition, certain types of condominium units are required to be registered with either the Office of Interstate Land Sales Registration of the Department of Housing and Urban Development, or the Securities and

Exchange Commission before any sales documents may be considered to be valid and binding. (See Chapter 4 for additional information on these regulations.)

All Conditions Precedent to Closing, Except
Completion of the Project, Must Be Performed

Completion of a project is generally required for recognizing a sale. Profit may, however, be recognized on the sale of a condominium unit on the percentage of completion method because of the long-term construction period. Most developers use the closing method. If the percentage of completion method is used, careful attention should be given to all factors involved in the closing process to determine that all conditions precedent to closing have been performed.

Declaration of Condominium. State laws require that a Declaration of Condominium be filed with the appropriate authorities before the seller can transfer title to the buyer. In many states, the filing of the Declaration is a perfunctory matter and developers often file the document only a short time before the first closing is scheduled to occur. In light of paragraph 14 of the *Profit Recognition Accounting Guide,* there is a question, when using the percentage of completion method of accounting, about whether the seller must file the Declaration before profit recognition is appropriate. While there are differences of opinion within the accounting profession, the following approach is representative of current practice:

- If the state law requires that the Declaration must be filed before a sales contract is binding and not voidable, then the Declaration must be filed before profit recognition is appropriate; and
- If the filing of the Declaration is a relatively routine matter and is not a prerequisite to a binding sales contract, then profit may be recognized in accordance with the percentage of completion method—provided that all other criteria for sale and profit recognition are met.

Permanent Financing. Sales contracts often include a condition that the seller is responsible for obtaining permanent financing for the buyer. In these circumstances, obtaining financing is a prerequisite to a sale for accounting purposes.

BUYER'S INVESTMENT IN
PURCHASED PROPERTY

Since uncertainty about collectibility of a receivable in a real estate sale may be greater than in other commercial transactions, a buyer's initial investment must be large enough to give the buyer a sufficient equity in the property so that the risk of loss through default motivates him to honor his obligation to a seller. As a result, the *Profit Recognition Accounting Guide* provides specific requirements for down payment and payment of the remaining balance of the purchase price. Although specific requirements for a buyer's investment may have been met, the requirement for a continuing evaluation of collectibility of receivables remains.

An Adequate Cash Down Payment Must Be Received by the Seller

Composition. The down payment must be composed of cash or the buyer's notes supported by an irrevocable letter of credit from an established lending institution. Any other consideration received, including securities and other personal property (such as paintings), qualifies as a down payment only at the time it is converted into cash without recourse to the seller.

In determining whether the down payment test has been met, any funds loaned or to be loaned to the buyer by the seller for any purpose, directly or indirectly, must first be deducted from the cash down payment.

Size. Paragraph 20 and Exhibit A of the *Profit Recognition Accounting Guide* set forth the minimum down payment, which would be the higher of (1) or (2) below:

1. *Exhibit A test (% of sales value):*
   Primary residence 5%
   Secondary or recreational residence 10%
   In the absence of specific evidence about the nature of use, 10% should be required.
2. *Alternate tests:*
   (a) If maximum financing exists, the down payment must be at

least equal to the excess of the sales value over 115 percent of the financing committed by the primary lender.

(b) If maximum financing is not arranged and the collection experience of the seller is not supported by reliable evidence, the down payment should not be less than 60 percent of the difference between the sales value and the financing available from loans of the type guaranteed by regulatory bodies or from independent financial institutions.

Leased Land.   If condominium units are sold subject to a lease of the underlying land from the seller/lessor to the buyer/lessee, the sales value (for the purpose of determining adequacy of the down payment) should include the present value of the lease payments receivable. This value should be computed at an appropriate interest or discount rate over the customary term of the indebtedness on the condominium units. The rate is the rate for primary debt if the lease is not subordinated or the rate for secondary debt if the lease is subordinate to loans with prior liens. (See page 123 on "Sales Subject to Land Lease" for profit recognition principles when a lease of land is involved.)

Inadequate Down Payment.   If the above down payment tests are not met, but the down payment received represents more than a deposit or option, the installment method may be used. The installment method apportions each cash collection between cost recovered and profit recognized in the same ratio as cost and profit are presumed to constitute the sales value. However, since the down payment requirements, described above, are already quite small, the profit to be recognized on the installment method would not normally be significant. Thus, the deposit method of accounting will usually be more practical in most circumstances until an adequate down payment is received.

The Buyer Must Be Required to Adequately Increase His Investment in the Property Annually

The buyer's commitment to pay the balance must be adequately secured. Typically, a condominium sales contract provides that the buyer pay the remaining balance at the time of closing. In such cases, the seller retains title to the property until closing and, therefore, no further security is normally required. However, if the seller provides the permanent financing, or a portion thereof, to the buyer, then such financing must be secured by property sold.

Paragraph 25 of the *Profit Recognition Accounting Guide* states that payments by the buyer must be:

> at least equal to the level annual payment that would be needed to pay the total indebtedness, including interest . . . over . . . the customary term of a first mortgage loan by an independent financial institution. . . .

It should be pointed out that down payments in excess of the minimum prescribed, as well as excess continuing payments, may be applied toward meeting the cumulative annual payments required in subsequent years.

The continuing investment requirement may cause particular problems for a high-rise developer if the period between the date of sale and closing is greater than one year and the minimum down payment is received. In such cases, this problem may be avoided by appropriately increasing the down payment requirements so that on a cumulative basis the first year's required payment test would be offset by the excess down payment. In lieu of requiring a higher down payment, the seller may:

1. use the deposit method and subsequently switch to the percentage of completion method after sufficient time has elapsed so that profit recognition occurs within one year of the date of closing; or
2. elect to use the closing method.

In those rare cases where the minimum annual payment requirements described above are not satisfied, but an adequate down payment is received, the seller may recognize a reduced profit by valuing the receivable at the present value of the lowest level of annual payments. Annual payments by the buyer, however, must be at least equal to annual level payments of principal and interest at an appropriate rate on applicable secondary indebtedness on the property.

In many cases, the balance of the purchase price due to the seller is expected to be paid from the proceeds of a loan to the buyer from an independent financial institution. When permanent financing is the responsibility of the buyer, reasonable assurance of collectibility may not be demonstrated (particularly in tight money periods) if permanent financing is not committed. At times, the seller is financially capable and willing to function as the long-term permanent lender. In these cases, collectibility must be demonstrated by an adequate review of the credit standing of the buyer that is similar to that which an independent lender would perform.

SELLER'S CONTINUED INVOLVEMENT
WITH PROPERTY SOLD

Although the seller must be concerned with general guidelines relating to continued involvement with the property sold, an option or obligation to repurchase the property is one type of involvement that is common in the sale of a condominium unit. Paragraph 56 of the *Profit Recognition Accounting Guide* states that no sale can be recognized if a seller has an obligation or an option to repurchase the property or the buyer has an option to compel the seller to repurchase the property. In most cases, the deposit method of accounting would be appropriate under these circumstances. A right of first refusal based on a bona fide offer by a third party is ordinarily not an obligation or an option to repurchase. Also, a commitment by the seller to assist the buyer or use his best efforts (with appropriate compensation) on a resale would not preclude profit recognition.

ADDITIONAL CRITERIA ESTABLISHED SPECIFICALLY FOR
USE OF THE PERCENTAGE OF COMPLETION METHOD

The sale of condominiums is unlike most other real estate sales transactions because individual single family units within a multi-family structure are normally sold individually. Condominium sales are analogous to a sale of a partial interest in real estate. Because of their unique characteristics, the *Profit Recognition Accounting Guide* in paragraph 60 sets forth certain specific requirements for recognizing profit on the sale of individual units in a condominium project:

> Single-family units in condominium projects are often sold individually. Recognizing a profit on the sale of individual units is often appropriate, provided the transaction meets all conditions for profit recognition at time of sale as to collectibility of sales price and ability to estimate costs not yet incurred. Profit should not be recognized, however, unless construction is beyond a preliminary stage, the buyer is committed to the

extent of being unable to require a refund, sufficient units have already been sold to assure that the property will not revert to rental property, and aggregate sales proceeds can be estimated reasonably. The profit to be recognized should be calculated on the basis of the percentage of completion of the project times the gross profit on the units sold. For this purpose, the project may be defined as a building, a group of buildings, a single structure or a complete project, depending on the circumstances.

The Developer Must Have the Ability to Estimate Costs Not Yet Incurred

The ability to estimate costs not yet incurred is a necessary condition for profit recognition. In determining whether or not this ability is present, consideration should be given to the prior experience of the developer, the type of construction contract, and the current economic conditions affecting the cost of construction and money. (Some guidance for estimation of future costs is set forth on page 110.)

A problem unique to condominium developers is support of the condominium association. As an inducement, the seller may at times guarantee that the monthly assessments to be charged to the buyers by the condominium association will not exceed a certain amount for a stated period of time or until a certain percentage of occupancy is obtained. In some circumstances, the costs of this support could be significant. In those instances, full deferral of profit until the guarantee lapses is appropriate when there is uncertainty about the cost of the guarantee.

Construction Must Be Beyond a Preliminary Stage

This requirement generally has been interpreted to mean that construction has started and is beyond the foundation stage of completion. There is some variance of practice in the method of determining the stage of completion for this test. Most often the stage of completion is based solely on direct construction costs; however, sometimes the stage of completion is based on direct construction costs plus the incurred portion of the allocated common costs such as land, land improvements, amenities, and related carrying costs. A general rule of thumb for this test would be that 25 percent to as much as 50 percent of total direct construction costs must be incurred and in place (not just on site), depending on the nature of the project, before profit recognition would be appropriate.

Sufficient Units Must Be Sold to Assure That
the Property Will Not Revert to Rental Property

In determining whether this requirement has been met, the following factors should be considered:

- Economic conditions;
- The history of the developer;
- State laws may require that a specified percent of units be sold before the Declaration of Condominium may be filed;
- Sale contracts may provide a buyer with the right of rescission until a specified percent of units are sold;
- Construction loans may require that a specified percent of units be sold before the lender will release any unit; and/or
- End loan financing commitments may provide that a specified percent of units be sold before the closing of any sale.

All of the above factors should be considered before profit recognition is determined to be appropriate. In the absence of other specific requirements, such as those imposed by state laws or financing agreements, many developers use a rule of thumb that 50 percent of the units must be sold.

The Developer Must Be Able to Reasonably
Estimate Aggregate Sales Proceeds

In determining whether this condition has been met, consideration should be given to sales volume, trends of unit prices, developer experience, geographical location, and environmental factors. In many cases, various units in a condominium project are difficult to sell, indicating that the pricing structure may not reflect true value. For example, some units may be improperly designed because of changes in market demand. Some units may not be as desirable as others because of their location or aesthetic factors. In these cases, consideration should be given to the fact that some of the remaining units may have to be sold at substantially reduced prices.

METHODS OF ACCOUNTING FOR PROFIT RECOGNITION

There are two alternative methods of accounting for profit recognition on condominium sales:

- Closing method—sales and related profit are generally recorded at the time of closing of each unit. This method is sometimes referred to as the completed contract method (see page 107); and
- Percentage of completion method—unit sales are generally recorded on the date of sale. However, profit is recognized as construction progresses on the project (see page 108).

The criteria for profit recognition, described in the previous section, must be met before recognition of profit would be appropriate under either method of accounting. If the conditions are not met, the deposit, installment, or cost recovery methods of accounting may be appropriate. (These methods are briefly described on page 132.)

There is a presumption in accounting literature in favor of the percentage of completion method of accounting for long-term projects where dependable estimates can be made. Similarly, there is a presumption that the closing method is the preferable method of accounting for either short-term projects or when a lack of dependable estimates or inherent unknowns causes forecasts to be doubtful. Therefore, economic conditions must be considered in selecting the method of accounting.

In economic periods of high inflation, low sales volume, and tight money coupled with high interest rates, significant questions may arise about the developer's ability to reliably estimate costs not yet incurred. In these circumstances, the closing method of accounting would be preferable for most new condominium projects. With respect to established projects, for which the percentage of completion method is used, the developer should continually review profit recognition procedures to see if they properly provide for the uncertainty inherent in the economic environment.

For profit recognition purposes under either method, the project may be defined as a building, group of buildings, a single structure or a complete project. The principal consideration in defining the project is cost accounting, that is, the ability of the developer to identify direct construction costs with individual segments of a development.

Sales Value.   In determining gross profit to be recognized under either method of accounting, it may be necessary, as previously indicated, to reduce the stated sales price for imputation of interest. Or, as set forth in paragraph 46 of the *Profit Recognition Accounting Guide,* it may be necessary to reduce the sales price for imputation of compensation when a sales contract includes an agreement requiring the seller to provide management or other services without compensation or at compensation below the prevailing rates.

Imputation of Interest.   In most condominium sales, an independent lender finances the transaction, with the seller being paid in full at time of closing. However, if the seller finances the unpaid balance of the sales price or any of it, imputation of interest may be required. *Accounting Principles Board Opinion No. 21,* "Interest on Receivables and Payables," states that when an interest rate is not stated or the stated interest rate is unreasonable, the carrying value should be adjusted to its present value. This is done by discounting all future payments on the notes, using an imputed rate of interest at the prevailing rates available for similar financing with independent financial institutions. A distinction must be made between first and second mortgage loans because the appropriate imputed rate for a second mortgage would normally be significantly higher than the rate for a first mortgage loan. An example illustrating imputation of interest is set forth in Table 7.6 on page 75.

When a sales contract provides that after title has passed, the seller must render management or other services—for compensation less than the prevailing rates for such services—the stated sales price must be adjusted accordingly to provide for fair compensation over the period the services are to be rendered. However, when a seller is to be compensated at prevailing rates for contracted services, say as a rental agent in a resort condominium project, no deferral of profit or adjustment to the sales value would be necessary.

Losses.   Under either method of accounting, if the total estimated costs exceed the estimated aggregate proceeds, the total anticipated loss should be charged to income in the period in which the loss becomes evident. This prevents anticipated losses from being deferred to future periods.

Closing Method

This method of accounting is widely used by developers who construct and sell townhouse or garden apartment condominiums which have relatively short periods. The principal advantage of the closing method is that profit recognition is based on actual costs which eliminates the need to rely on estimates. However, in the case of developments with longer construction cycles, this method may result in profit being recognized at irregular intervals while the activity proceeds at a fairly even pace.

Under this method all payments or deposits received prior to recording the sale are generally accounted for as a liability until the exchange transaction is completed. Selling costs directly related to units sold may be deferred until the sale is recorded and profit is recognized, rather than being charged to income as incurred. Care should be taken, however, to avoid deferring excessive selling costs.

In situations where the seller has not completed construction of common areas—such as recreational facilities—or has guaranteed the amount of the monthly assessments to be charged by the condominium association (more fully described on page 94), the earnings process is not complete. Accordingly, a certain portion of the profit should be deferred even though the closing has occurred and the sale is recorded. The profit to be recognized upon closing of a dwelling unit should be based on the relationship of the costs already incurred to the total estimated costs. Costs to be factored into this determination should include the dwelling unit's allocated share of both direct construction costs and common costs. (See page 110 for Estimated Future Costs to Complete.)

Condominiums Sold Under Time-Sharing Concept. Some developers sell undivided interests in each of the individual units to two or more buyers with restrictions on the periods of time in which each buyer may occupy the unit. The completed contract method of accounting would seem warranted in such situations, at least until the developer has demonstrated the viability and success of the project being marketed. Profit on the accrual or installment method generally should not be recognized until all undivided interests for a given unit are sold and closed. However, the cost recovery method of accounting might be utilized in appropriate circumstances.

Percentage of Completion Method

This method of accounting has been adopted principally by developers constructing mid-rise or high-rise condominiums when the period of the construction cycle may extend up to two to three years. The principal advantage of this method is that it allows recognition of some profit as construction proceeds on units sold. However, this method requires heavy reliance on estimates of aggregate project costs and revenues—estimates which are, of course, subject to uncertainties.

Under the percentage of completion method, the profit to be recognized should be calculated on the basis of the percentage of completion of the project times the gross profit on the units sold. Either of the following alternatives may be used:

- Actual stage of direct construction as determined through architectural or engineering studies; or
- The relationship of costs already incurred to total estimated costs to be incurred. Total costs would properly include direct construction costs and the allocated share of common costs such as site improvements and amenities. Practice is divided, however, including other common costs such as land, predevelopment costs, and construction interest, if capitalized. The costs selected for inclusion should be those that most clearly reflect the earnings process. (Page 110 for Future Costs to Complete.)

An example illustrating the percentage of completion method is set forth in Table 9.1.

CONDOMINIUM CONVERSIONS

The conversion of rental property to condominiums has become prevalent in the last few years in many areas of the country. For the developer converting rental property into a condominium, the accounting principles with respect to accounting for profit recognition on sales of converted

Table 9.1. Percentage of Completion Method

Assumptions

The developer is building a garden-type condominium project. The project consists of 15 buildings in clusters of 3 buildings to a cluster and 6 units to a building. Amenities are common to all 15 buildings (5 clusters). Amenities are well defined and are all contracted out. They are 75% complete at year-end. Assume a minimum construction standard of 35% and a minimum sales standard of 50% for profit recognition. The sales price of each unit is $30,000. Estimated gross profit per unit is $5,000.

For purposes of income recognition, it has been agreed that a cluster (but not a building) constitutes the project. By year-end, the sales and development activity was:

	Units sold	Percentage of completion
Cluster A		
Building 1	6	95%
Building 2	6	90%
Building 3	3	25%
	15–(83%)	70%
Cluster B		
Building 1	4	60%
Building 2	2	20%
Building 3	2	10%
	8–(44%)	30%
To date	23	50%

The percentage of completion was determined based on the ratio of direct construction costs incurred to the total construction contract amounts on an individual building basis. The ratio was also verified with a physical inspection by the developer's engineering staff.

Profit to be Recognized by Year-End

Cluster A—70% × 15 × $5000	$52,500
Cluster B—("Project" not 35% complete or 50% sold)	None
Total	$52,500

units are the same as the principles for the sale of new units. All criteria for recognition of profit must be met.

Depending upon the circumstances, one of the two profit recognition accounting methods, either the closing method or the percentage of completion method, would be appropriate. The closing method of accounting is predominantly used in practice.

In a conversion, a significant number of units may be sold to existing tenants. Such sales may not be indicative of the ultimate success of the project and, therefore, care should be exercised in establishing the percentage of units which must be sold before profit recognition is considered appropriate.

The percentage of completion method is seldom used for profit recognition in a condominium conversion. If used, however, the stage of completion should be determined on the basis of costs incurred compared to total estimated costs to be incurred. In any calculation of the percentage of completion or another method of deferral of income, there is a problem in determining which costs should be included. In a conversion development, the selling and interest costs could exceed the direct conversion cost. Logically, all selling, interest, and direct conversion costs—including any capitalized losses of rental operations—would be factored into the determination of percentage of completion for income recognition.

ESTIMATED FUTURE COSTS TO COMPLETE

Future costs to complete must be estimated under either the closing method or the percentage of completion method. In addition, the estimation of future costs to complete is necessary for determining the net realizable value of unsold units. Estimated future costs should be based on adequate architectural and engineering studies and should include reasonable provisions for:

- Unforeseen costs in accordance with sound cost estimation practices;
- Anticipated cost inflation in the construction industry;
- The costs of offsite improvements, utility facilities and amenities, to the extent that they will not be recovered from outside third parties;
- Operating losses of utility operations and recreational and club facilities. These losses would be expected to be incurred for a relatively

limited period of time—usually prior to sale of the facilities or transfer to some public authority; and

- Any other guaranteed support arrangements or activities to the extent that they will not be recovered from outside third parties or be borne by a future purchaser. (For example, a developer may agree to support the association to ensure that the monthly common assessments to the buyers will not exceed a stated minimum amount for a period of time.)

Estimates of amounts to be recovered from any sources should be discounted to present value as of the date the related costs are expected to be incurred.

REVISIONS OF ESTIMATED FUTURE COSTS

Estimated costs to complete construction should be reviewed, at least annually, through updated architectural and engineering studies and appropriate adjustments should be made. Adjustments to estimated costs to complete construction of a project should not be accounted for by restating amounts previously reported but should be accounted for in (a) the period of change if the change affects that period only; or (b) the period of change and future periods if the change affects both. The application of the principle, however, requires interpretation as there appear to be two acceptable alternatives.

The AICPA *Audit Guide: Audits of Construction Contractors,* which predates *Accounting Principles Board Opinion No. 20,* recommends on page 15:

income to be recognized in a contractor's accounts be either:

(a) that percentage of estimated total income that incurred costs to date bear to estimated total costs after giving effect to estimates of costs to complete based upon most recent information, or

(b) that percentage of estimated total income that may be indicated by such other measure of progress toward completion as may be appropriate having due regard to work performed.

Based on this guideline, cumulative income should be adjusted based either on current estimated costs or progress toward completion. The difference between cumulative income and income previously reported would be recorded as the current year's income (or loss).

Alternatively, the *Retail Land Accounting Guide* provides the following guidelines in paragraph 41:

> Adjustments of estimated costs to complete improvements and amenities of a project will not affect previously recorded deferred revenues applicable to future improvements and should not be charged or credited to income of the period in which the need for adjustment becomes evident unless the adjusted total exceeds the applicable deferred revenue. . . . When cost estimates are revised, the relationship of the two elements included in deferred revenue—costs and profit—should be recalculated on a cumulative basis to determine future income recognition as performance takes place.

Based on this guideline, no adjustment would be made for income recorded in prior years. The income to be recorded in the period of the change in estimate and future periods would be based on the revised estimated costs. Naturally, if the total adjusted costs to complete exceed deferred sales revenue, the total anticipated loss should be charged to income in the period in which the need for adjustment becomes evident. This method also appears to be an acceptable accounting practice.

Sales Subject to Land Lease

Occasionally, condominium units are sold subject to a lease of the underlying land. Normally in this situation the land is owned or leased by the developer/seller and the buyer executes a lease agreement with the developer/seller. There is an accounting problem inherent in this type of transaction. It is impractical to distinguish between the profit on the sale of the condominium units and the profit under the related lease of land because the results are interdependent. The accounting for sales subject to a land lease is set forth in paragraphs 30 to 33 of the *Profit Recognition Accounting Guide*.

The computation of the required down payment must be adjusted to reflect the inclusion of the land lease in the sales value of the improvements. (See page 123 for additional information.)

Chapter 10

Special Accounting Problems

There are a number of other areas in accounting for sales of real estate that are unique and require special accounting rules. This chapter will deal with these areas. They include accounting for construction contracts, retail land sales, sales subject to land lease, sales of options, sales to limited partnerships, nonmonetary transactions, and income tax considerations.

CONSTRUCTION CONTRACTS

Although most real estate developers acquire land in order to develop and construct improvements for their own use or for sale to others, some develop and construct improvements for others. There are also many general contractors whose principal business is developing and constructing improvements for others and rarely, if ever, own the land.

This section covers accounting guidelines for development and construction contracts where the contractor does not own the land but is providing such services for others. The principal matter concerning accounting for construction contracts is when to record income. Construction contracts are generally of two types: fixed price and cost-plus. Under fixed price contracts, a contractor agrees to perform services for a fixed amount. Although the contract price is fixed, it may frequently be revised as a result of change orders as construction proceeds. If the contract is longer than a few months, the contractor usually receives advances from the customer as construction progresses.

Cost-plus contracts are employed in a variety of forms, such as cost plus a percentage of cost or cost plus a fixed fee. Sometimes defined costs may be limited and penalties provided in situations where stated maximum costs are exceeded. Under cost-plus agreements, the contractor is usually reimbursed for his costs as costs are incurred and, in addition, is paid a specified fee. In most cases a portion of the fee is retained until the construction is completed and accepted. The method of recording income under cost-plus type contracts generally is the same as for fixed price contracts and is described below.

Methods of Accounting

Short-term contracts generally pose few accounting problems because income is usually recognized when construction is substantially completed and accepted. Long-term contracts, on the other hand, present special problems because they often continue over several accounting periods. There are two generally accepted methods of accounting for long-term contracts:

- *Percentage of completion method* is preferable when it is possible to make reasonably dependable estimates and all of the following conditions exist:
    - The contract is clear about the goods or services to be provided, the consideration to be exchanged, and the manner and terms of settlement.
    - The buyer can be expected to pay for the services performed.
    - The contractor can be expected to perform his contractual obligations.
- *Completed contract method* is preferable when lack of dependable estimates or inherent hazards cause forecasts to be doubtful.

It is possible that a contractor may use one method for some contracts and the other for other contracts. There is no inconsistency since consistency in application lies in using the same accounting treatment for the same set of conditions from one accounting period to another. The method used, and circumstances when it is used, should be disclosed in the accounting policy footnote to the financial statements. It should be noted that estimates of revenues, costs, and stage of completion are the primary criteria and that billings are generally not a suitable basis for income recognition; billings may have no real relationship to performance.

The current authoritative literature on accounting for construction contracts is comprised of AICPA *Accounting Research Bulletin No. 45,* "Long-Term Construction-Type Contracts" and the AICPA *Industry Audit Guide,* "Audits of Construction Contractors." Most of the principles described herein are based on this authoritative literature. Note, however, that the AICPA issued in December 1979 an Exposure Draft of a proposed Statement of Position on "Accounting for Performance of Construction-Type and Certain Production-Type Contracts," as well as an Exposure Draft of an "Audit and Accounting Guide for Construction Contractors," which incorporates the accounting provisions of the Statement of Position. Issuance of a final Statement of Position may change some of the accounting practices described herein.

Under the proposed Statement of Position the use of the completed contract method would be severely curtailed. It indicates that there must be specific, persuasive, and documented evidence of inherent hazards to justify departure from the use of the percentage of completion method. It further states that in circumstances where it is not possible to estimate the ultimate outcome of the contract, except to assure that no loss will be incurred, zero profit should be estimated and revenue recognized equal to costs incurred.

Percentage of Completion Method

This generally preferred method recognizes income on work as a contract progresses. *Accounting Research Bulletin No. 45,* in paragraph 4, states:

> that the recognized income be that percentage of estimated total income, either:
> (a) that incurred costs to date bear to estimated total costs after giving effect to estimates of costs to complete based upon most recent information, or
> (b) that may be indicated by such other measure of progress toward completion as may be appropriate having due regard to work performed.

One generally accepted method of measuring progress is the stage of construction as determined through engineering or architectural studies.

Based on this guideline, the difference between cumulative income and income previously recorded should be recorded in the current year's income.

Under the costs incurred method, there may be certain costs that should be excluded from the calculation. For example, substantial quantities of standard materials not unique to the project may have been delivered to the job site but not yet utilized; or engineering and architectural fees incurred may represent 20 percent of total estimated costs even though only ten percent of the construction has been performed.

The principal advantage of the percentage of completion method is the current recognition of income on the uncompleted contracts through the use of current estimates of costs to complete or of progress toward completion. The principal disadvantage is that it is necessarily dependent upon estimates of ultimate costs, which are subject to the uncertainties frequently inherent in long-term contracts.

Completed Contract Method

The completed contract method recognizes income only when a contract is completed or substantially completed, such as when the remaining costs to be incurred are not significant. Under this method, costs and billings are reflected in the balance sheet, but there are no charges or credits to the income statement.

It may be appropriate to allocate general and administrative expenses to contract costs rather than periodic income in situations where there are only a few contracts and no contracts are completed in a specific period. This may result in a better matching of costs and revenues.

There should not be any excessive deferral of general or administrative costs, such as may occur if total overhead were allocated to contracts when construction volume is low. In this situation, only a reasonable allocation should be made to capitalized costs; the remaining costs should be shown as period expenses, even if a loss results.

The principal advantage of the completed contract method is that it is based on results as finally determined, rather than on estimates for unperformed work that may involve unforeseen costs and possible losses. The principal disadvantage is that it does not reflect current performance when the period of the contract extends into more than one accounting period. Under these circumstances, it may result in irregular recognition of income.

Provision for Losses

Under either of the above methods, provision should be made for the entire loss on the contract in the period when current estimates of total contract costs indicate a loss. The provision for loss should represent the best judgment that can be made under the circumstances.

Ordinarily, a provision for loss on a contract should not be necessary unless the total estimated contract costs are expected to exceed the total contract price. Other factors that should be considered in arriving at the projected loss on a contract include target penalties for late completion and rewards for early completion, nonreimbursable costs on cost-plus contracts, and the effects of change orders. When using the completed contract method and allocating general and administrative expenses to contract costs, total general and administrative expenses that are expected to be allocated to the contract are to be considered together with other estimated contract costs.

SALES OF RETAIL LAND

The dominant activity of the retail land sales industry is retail marketing of numerous lots, subdivided from a larger parcel of land. These lots are used by the original or a subsequent purchaser as a primary or secondary homesite or as a recreational property for motor homes or other recreational vehicles. The AICPA *Accounting Guide: Accounting for Retail Land Sales,* called the *Retail Land Guide,* covers this unique segment of the real estate industry. Its provisions, summarized below, have been generally accepted as the appropriate practices to be followed.

Scope of Retail Land Guide

The *Retail Land Guide* applies to retail lot sales on a volume basis with down payments that are less than those required to evaluate collectibility of casual sales of real estate. Wholesale or bulk sales of land and retail sales from projects comprising a small number of lots are subject to the general principles for profit recognition on real estate sales. The guide further indicates in paragraph 9 that, where retail land is sold in an improved state with a down payment of ten percent or more accompanied by a general obligation note receivable (secured by a first mortgage and marketable at banks without substantial discount and without recourse to the seller), many provisions of the guide do not apply because the earnings process is complete.

Criteria for Recording a Sale

Sales should not be recorded until:

- The period of cancellation with refund has expired and the customer has made all required payments;
- Aggregate payments (including interest) equal or exceed ten percent of contract sales price; or
- The selling company is clearly capable of providing all improvements and offsite facilities promised.

If these conditions are met, either the accrual or the installment method must be selected. If the conditions are not met, the deposit method of accounting discussed on page 132 should be used.

Criteria for Accrual Method

These tests for using the accrual method should be applied on a project-by-project basis:

- The properties clearly must be useful for residential or recreational purposes at the end of the normal payment period;
- The project's improvements must have progressed beyond preliminary stages, and there is evidence that the work will be completed according to plan;
- The receivable cannot be subject to subordination to new loans on the property, except subordination for home construction purposes under certain conditions; and

- The collection experience for the project must indicate that collectibility of receivable balances is reasonably predictable and that 90
  percent of the contracts in force six months after sales are recorded
  will be collected in full. Alternatively, down payments are sufficient
  to record the sale if it were a casual sale—say 20 to 25 percent of
  sales price.

In order to predict collection results of current sales, there must be satis-
factory experience on prior sales of the type of land currently being sold
in the project. In addition the collection period must be long enough to
reasonably estimate the percentage of sales that will be fully collected. In
a new project, the developers' experience on other prior projects may be
used, if they have demonstrated an ability to successfully develop other
projects and the other projects clearly had the same characteristics (environment, clientele, contract terms, sales methods) as the new project.

Collection and cancellation experience within a project may differ with
varying types of sales methods—such as telephone sales, broker sales, and
site visitation sales. Accordingly, historical data should be maintained with
respect to each type of sales method used.

Unless all conditions for the use of the accrual method are met for the
entire project, the installment method of accounting should be applied to
all recorded sales of the project.

Accounting Procedures—Accrual Method

The following general procedures should be used to account for revenues
and costs under the accrual method of accounting:

- Record sales contracts at the gross amount;
- Discount receivables to reflect an appropriate interest rate;
- Establish an allowance for contract cancellation;
- Defer revenues based on the ratio of future costs to be incurred to the
  total costs—deferred revenue should be recognized as development is
  performed; and
- Calculate the cost of sales only on the net sales recorded after elimi-
  nating the sales expected to be cancelled before maturity.

Interest Rate

The *Retail Land Guide* states that:

> . . . the effective annual yield on the receivable . . . should not be less than the minimum annual rate charged locally by commercial banks and established retail organizations to borrowers financing purchases of consumer personal property with installment credit. In the absence of more definitive criteria, the objective of evaluating the gross receivable less contract cancellation allowance should be to record the net receivable at the value at which it could be sold on a volume basis at the time of the initial transaction without recourse to the seller.

According to the guide, for 1972 and prior years, a rate of not less than 12 percent is appropriate. A 1979 survey of reports on major retail land developers indicated that all developers using the accrual method discounted receivables to yield an effective interest rate of 12 percent.

Delinquency and Cancellation

Paragraph 27 of the *Retail Land Guide* states:

> Evaluating historical data to establish the ability to predict the collection of receivables from current sales requires experience with a representative sample of receivables over an adequate period of time. If receivables in the sample are past due at the end of the period of time selected, the Committee concludes that the receivables should be considered uncollectible and the contracts presumed to be cancelled (for this purpose) if regular payments due are unpaid for the following delinquency periods:

Percent of contract price paid	Delinquency period
Less than 25%	90 days
25% but less than 50%	120 days
50% and over	150 days

The historical data should, of course, be continually updated and an allowance for contract cancellations should be adjusted accordingly to reflect any changes.

Deferral of Revenues Related to Future Performance

Unless all improvements and amenities for which the seller is obligated are complete, a portion of the revenues must be deferred until completion. The deferral should be based on the ratio of costs yet to be incurred to the total costs. The total cost in the denominator should include costs previously expensed, such as costs for interest and marketing.

An example illustrating the application of the accrual method is set forth in Table 10.1.

Accounting Procedures—Installment Method

If the criteria for recording a sale have been met but the criteria for the use of the accrual method are not satisfied, the installment method is required. The following general procedures should be used to account for revenues and costs under the installment method:

- The entire contract price should be reported as revenue in the year of sale. A market rate of interest need not be imputed;
- Cost of sales (including a provision for future improvement costs to be incurred) and selling costs should be charged to income in the current period;
- Gross profit less selling costs directly associated with the project should be deferred and recognized in income as payments of principal are received on the sales contract receivable; and
- Selling costs to be deducted in determining the gross profit to be deferred above should be limited to the amounts expected to be recovered from collectible contracts.

Change to Accrual Method from Installment Method

When all conditions for use of the accrual method are satisfied on a project previously accounted for under the installment method, a change should be made to the accrual method of accounting for the entire project. The effect should be accounted for as a change in accounting estimate due to changed circumstances in accordance with the provisions of AICPA

Table 10.1. Retail Land Sales—Application of Accrual Method

Assumptions

1. Gross sales contracts of $1000 are recorded with a stated interest rate of 6% per annum. Down payments of $100 relative to these contracts are received.
2. Uncollectible contracts are estimated to be $100 and are reduced by estimated forfeited down payments of $10. Net allowance is $90.
3. Costs applicable to sales contracts of $900 (gross sales less estimated uncollectibles) are:
   Land—$60, selling expenses—$300, development costs to date—$40 and future improvement costs—$100.
4. Minimum annual yield required on contracts receivable is 12%.

Discount required

Sales contracts receivable (gross contracts of $1000 less down payments of $100 and net allowance for uncollectible contracts of $90)	$	810
Present value of 108 level monthly payments of $9.72 on sales contracts receivable, discounted at 12%		640
Discount required	$	170

Computation of deferred revenue applicable to future improvements
Future improvement costs divided by total costs to be incurred, times gross sales net of interest discount and estimated cancellations

$$\frac{\$100}{\$60 + \$300 + \$40 + \$100} \times (\$1000 - 170 - 100) = \qquad \$ \quad 146$$

Profit recognition under accrual method

Gross revenues	$	1000
Less: Estimated uncollectible sales		90
Deferred revenue applicable to future improvements		146
Valuation discount		170
Net revenues	$	594
Less: Costs and expenses incurred ($60 + 300 + 40)		400
Pretax income	$	194

122

Accounting Principles Board Opinion No. 20, "Accounting Changes," paragraphs 31–33. It should be pointed out that the problems involved in evaluating adequacy of collection experience make it very difficult to determine a precise time at which the change is appropriate.

SALES SUBJECT TO LAND LEASE

Occasionally, property is sold subject to a lease of the underlying land. In this situation the land usually is owned or leased by the developer/seller and the buyer executes a lease agreement with the developer/seller. In some sales, however, the buyer assumes a land lease with a third-party lessor.

This situation requires particular attention to the substance, as opposed to the form, of the transaction. Both the sale and the lease usually involve level payments by the buyer/lessee over an extended period. Under the sale, title to the improvements technically passes to the buyer, but it, of course, reverts to the lessor as a leasehold improvement when the lease term expires. On the other hand, the residual value of the land (and the improvements) at lease termination may be largely conjectural or, when discounted to present value, may be nominal because of the length of the lease—the transaction may pass substantially all the attributes of ownership to the buyer/lessee.

The *Profit Recognition Accounting Guide* states that it is impractical to distinguish between the profit on the sale and the profit under the related lease of the land because the results are interdependent. Under paragraphs 30 to 33, the sale and lease are treated essentially as a single transaction as described below.

Down Payment Test

The computation of the required down payment for profit recognition on the sale requires an adjustment to include the land lease in the sales value of the improvements. In this situation, sales value must include the present value of lease payments for the term of the primary debt on the improvements.

Computatiòn of Profit

The computation of profit must give consideration to whether the seller owns the land or leases the land from a third party.

Seller Owns Land.   The general rule is that profit to be recognized on sale of the improvements should be computed by deducting the sum of the cost of the improvements and the cost of the land from the sum of sales value of the improvements and the present value of the lease payments and should not be in excess of the cost of the land, over the customary term of the primary indebtedness. The present value of the lease payments should be computed at an appropriate interest or discount rate. The rate to be used is the rate for primary debt if the lease is not subordinated, or the rate for secondary debt if the lease is subordinated to loans with prior liens.

The result of this method of computing profit is to write off all costs, including the cost of the land. No consideration is given to:

- The residual value of land;
- The residual value of rentals on land after the customary term of the primary indebtedness; or
- The profit inherent in the land lease where the present value of lease payments over the customary term exceeds the cost of the land.

An example illustrating the computation of profit is set forth in Table 10.2.

Seller Leases Land from Third Party/Owner.   If the seller's lease obligation to a third party/owner is assumed by the buyer and the seller has no further obligations under the land lease, the amount of profit to be recognized is not affected. The timing, though, may be affected because the lease must be considered in evaluating the adequacy of the down payment.

If the seller's lease obligation is not assumed by the buyer, the amount of profit recognized by the seller should be reduced by any loss inherent in the sublease. The loss is the excess of the present value of lease payments to be paid by the seller over the present value of sublease payments

Table 10.2.   Computation of Profit on Sales Subject to Leaseback

The following is a simple illustration of a lease between a seller/lessor and the buyer/lessee:		
Down payment		$ 205,000
Balance of existing first mortgage payable by seller but assumed by buyer, 28 year term		760,000
Second mortgage payable to seller, 12% interest		50,000
Sales value before effect of land lease		1,015,000
99 year land lease—$11,580 per year—payable monthly in advance—present value of 336 monthly payments discounted at 12% (imputed interest rate for second lien receivable)		94,000
Adjusted sales value		1,109,000
Assume—cost of improvements	700,000	
cost of land	150,000	850,000
Profit		$ 259,000

The effect of adding the present value of lease payments ($94,000) to the sales value and deducting all costs of land ($150,000) is a reduction in profit of $56,000 from $315,000 to $259,000. The adjusted sales value of $1,109,000 would be used to determine whether the down payment test has been met.

the seller is to receive from the buyer. Profit inherent in the land sublease (where sublease payments to be received from the buyer exceed those that must be paid by the seller) should be deferred and realized as accrued under the lease.

FAS 13.   While the *Profit Recognition Accounting Guide* predates the *Statement of Financial Accounting Standards No. 13* (FAS 13), "Accounting for Leases," issued in November 1976, FAS 13 prevails if the two documents conflict. It does not specifically deal with sales subject to land leases but paragraphs 25, 26 and 105 set forth rules for leases involving land only and leases involving land and buildings. The thrust of FAS 13 is that:

• A lease of land should always be accounted for as an operating lease unless it is in substance an installment purchase; and

- A single lease of land and buildings should be fragmented for classification and recording between land and building elements. To reduce the practical problems, FAS 13 requires this fragmentation
  only when the fair value of the land is 25 percent or more of the total fair value of the leased property at the inception of the lease.
  This could be deemed to be contrary to the *Profit Recognition Accounting Guide*'s requirement that the two transactions—the sale and
  the lease—be accounted for as a single transaction.

There appears to be no conflict that the lease be considered in determining whether the down payment test has been met. It is possible, however, that the guidelines for measuring profit on the sale conflict with, and
are overridden by, FAS 13. Potential conflicts between these two documents will have to be resolved—perhaps by the FASB issuing an interpretation—as they arise.

SALE OF AN OPTION

A sale of an option to purchase real estate is a sale of an interest in real
estate. The question of accounting for options related to interests in real
estate is covered in the AICPA *Statement of Position 75–6* as follows:

Sale of Option by Option Holder

For purposes of evaluating the buyer's commitment when an option is
sold by an option holder, the initial and continuing investment by the
buyer of the option (which would exclude amounts which are subject to
refund by the seller) should be related to the total of the exercise price
of the option and the sales price of the option. For example, if the option
is sold for $150,000 ($50,000 cash and a $100,000 note) and the exer-
cise price is $500,000, the sales value against which the buyer's down
payment and continuing investment is measured is $650,000. If the
buyer's investment is inadequate, income may be recorded on the cost
recovery method to the extent nonrefundable cash proceeds exceed the
seller's cost of the option.

Sale of Option by Property Owner

Proceeds from the issuance of a real estate option by a property owner
should be accounted for as a deposit as set forth under Paragraph 35 of
the *Profit Recognition Accounting Guide*. It is not appropriate to recog-

nize income before the option either expires or is exercised because the sale of the option cannot be evaluated independently from the sale of the real estate to which the option relates. If the option is exercised, cash proceeds from the issuance of the option should be accounted for as a down payment and included in sales value.

SALES TO LIMITED PARTNERSHIPS

In recent years, sales to limited partnerships have been very common, particularly regarding operating properties when the buyer is looking for a tax shelter. Many of these sales present significant accounting problems not only because the buyer is a limited partnership and collection of any receivable may be dependent upon operations of the property, but also because the seller frequently has continuing involvement with the buyer or the property sold. This requires (a) deferral of sale recognition, (b) full deferral of profit, or (c) spreading of the profit.

It should be pointed out, however, that full profit recognition on sales to limited partnerships would not be prohibited if all requirements for profit recognition are met. During the sale of an operating property, for example, if there is no continuing involvement of the seller other than an insignificant receivable (defined as less than 15 percent of maximum first lien financing available), and the tests on the adequacy of the buyer's initial down payment and his continuing investment are met, full profit may be recognized. A significant receivable, however, usually constitutes continuing seller involvement because collection of the receivable is frequently dependent on the operations of the property.

Frequent Problems Encountered in Sales to Limited Partnerships.   A seller's continuing involvement presents some very complex problems. This section sets forth some of the more common problems on sales to limited partnerships, either individually or in combination. They are listed below together with page references to the discussion of the respective accounting issues when the seller:

- Is a general partner in a limited partnership holding the property and holds a significant receivable (defined as 15 percent of maximum first lien financing available) from the buyer/limited partnership—the sale must be deferred (see page 78).

- Is a general or limited partner in the limited partnership and has granted preferences as to profits or cash flow to other investors—the cost recovery method is required (see page 90).

- Is required to support operations via such means as guarantees and leaseback arrangements—the sale and/or profit must be deferred (see pages 80 to 83).

- Is responsible for developing or constructing improvements on the property—profit must be spread over improvement period (see page 83).

- Has an option or obligation to repurchase the property—the sale must be deferred (see page 77).

- Is required to arrange or provide financing for the project—the sale must be deferred (see page 80).

- Retains an equity interest in the buyer/limited partnership—all or a portion of the property sold frequently must be deferred (see page 91).

- Retains an equity interest in the property—the profit relating to the portion of the property sold frequently must be deferred (see page 90).

- Holds a significant receivable (as defined) from the buyer and collection is dependent upon operations of the property—the profit frequently must be deferred and/or spread over a presumed support period (see page 78).

- Has a management contract with the buyer without adequate compensation—the sales value and profit must be reduced (see page 83).

- Has a noncancellable management contract with the buyer providing compensation on terms unusual for the services to be rendered—the profit is frequently required to be deferred and/or spread over a presumed support period (see page 87).

ACCOUNTING FOR NONMONETARY TRANSACTIONS

Occasionally, investors and others will exchange real estate owned to others for property that they own. Sometimes little cash is exchanged and the transaction is essentially nonmonetary. The principles of accounting for nonmonetary transactions are set forth in AICPA *Accounting Principles Board Opinion No. 29*. In general, noncash real estate exchanges rarely result in recognition of profit.

The basic principle is that accounting for nonmonetary transactions should be based on the fair value of the real estate exchanged (same basis as that used in monetary transactions). This principle has been modified for situations where (1) fair value is not determinable within reasonable limits, and (2) the earnings process is not culminated. Such circumstances are typical in nonmonetary real estate exchanges.

Regarding this second modification, the opinion states:

> the following two types of nonmonetary exchange transactions do not culminate an earnings process:
> (a) An exchange of . . . property held for sale in the ordinary course of business for . . . property to be sold in the same line of business to facilitate sales to customers other than the parties to the exchange, and
> (b) An exchange of a productive asset not held for sale in the ordinary course of business for a similar productive asset or an equivalent interest in the same or similar productive asset . . .

If the exchange is not, essentially, the culmination of an earning process, accounting for an exchange of real estate should be based on the recorded amount of the real estate transferred.

This would seem to eliminate profit recognition on most nonmonetary real estate exchanges. However, when one party purchases a property for monetary consideration and simultaneously exchanges that property for another, profit recognition would seem to be appropriate because the transaction is essentially monetary.

Although practice is not settled, transactions involving exchanges of properties—such as manufacturing plants and headquarters buildings for certain other real estate investments such as raw land and apartments— may qualify for income recognition.

INCOME TAX CONSIDERATIONS

Although there are particular accounting guidelines for financial reporting purposes, statutory requirements and other considerations will create different tax accounting methods for many developments. Income tax regulations require that a taxpayer use the same method of accounting as he uses for keeping his books, provided the Internal Revenue Commissioner believes the method clearly reflects income. Thus, the developer may be allowed to use the cash method, the accrual method or some other method of accounting. Once a method of accounting is elected for tax purposes, it generally may not be changed without prior approval from the Internal Revenue Service.

Here are a few basic tax rules, some of which may differ from accounting rules.

Time for Recording a Sale.   For tax purposes an arm's length sale is generally deemed to have occurred either when title passes or when possession and the benefit and burden of ownership pass to the buyer. Normally, both criteria are satisfied at the time of closing.

Time for Recognizing Profit (or Loss).   In general, profit must be recognized for tax purposes at the time of sale despite the presence of many criteria that will preclude recognition of revenue and profit for financial reporting purposes. For tax purposes there are no minimum down payment requirements, no limitations as to the type of security provided by the buyer, no minimum acceptable terms on any unpaid balance of the purchase price, nor any restrictions on subordination. The existence of future obligations to repurchase or to complete amenities will not preclude recognition of profit at the time of sale for tax purposes.

The principal exception to the rule requiring profit recognition for tax purposes at the time of sale is when the developer elects, under appropriate tax rules, to defer profit by reporting it on the installment method. When the percentage of completion method is used, income relating to performance may be recognized for accounting purposes upon execution of a contract to sell. However, no portion of any payment received pursuant to the contract would ordinarily be taxable upon receipt since the criteria necessary for recording the sale for tax purposes, as described previously, would not be met.

Measuring Profit.   For tax purposes, sales proceeds are not reduced to reflect imputed interest unless the stated rate of interest is less than four percent simple interest per annum. If imputation is required, it will be done in accordance with income tax regulations and may vary from the result obtained for financial reporting purposes.

Estimated costs to complete are allowed as current costs of sale for tax purposes—providing the developer is bound by a contractual obligation or legal requirement to incur those costs and if they are determinable with reasonable accuracy. Moreover, where a sale has occurred, the inability to estimate costs to complete does not preclude reporting the gross proceeds as revenue for tax purposes.

The timing differences between financial accounting and tax accounting are numerous. These differences should be carefully analyzed and accounted for in accordance with *Accounting Principles Board Opinion No. 11,* "Accounting for Income Taxes."

Chapter 11

Alternative Methods of Accounting

Although the *Profit Recognition Accounting Guide* indicates that in some circumstances the accrual method of accounting is not appropriate and other methods of accounting may be used, it does not always indicate what method should be used or how it should be applied. It is often very difficult, therefore, to determine the appropriate method to use and whether alternative methods are acceptable.

The methods prescribed where the buyer's initial or continuing investment is inadequate:

- Deposit
- Installment
- Cost recovery

This chapter is consistent with AICPA *Statement of Position 78–4,* "Application of the Deposit, Installment, and Cost Recovery Methods in Accounting for Sales of Real Estate."

The methods prescribed for transactions that cannot be considered a sale as a result of seller's continuing involvement:

- Financing
- Lease
- Profit sharing (or co-venture)

DEPOSIT METHOD

When the substance of a real estate transaction indicates that a sale has not occurred for accounting purposes as a result of the buyer's inadequate investment, recognition of the sale should be deferred and the deposit method used until the conditions requiring its use no longer exist. For example, when the down payment is so small that the substance of the transaction is an option arrangement, the sale should not be recorded.

Accounting Procedures

Accounting under the deposit method is described in paragraph 35 of the *Profit Recognition Accounting Guide:*

> The deposit method postpones recognizing a sale until a determination can be made as to whether a sale has occurred for accounting purposes. Pending recognition of the sale, the seller records no receivable but continues to show in his financial statements the property and related existing debt and discloses the status of the property. Cash received from the buyer is reported as a deposit on the contract except that portions of cash received that are designated by the contract as interest and are not subject to refund may appropriately offset carrying charges (property taxes and interest on existing debt) on the property.

Except as indicated in the last sentence above, all cash received—including down payments and principal and interest payments by the buyer to the seller—should be reported as a deposit (liability). Related accounting and financial presentation matters are:

- Notes receivable arising from the transaction should not be recorded.
- The property and any related mortgage debt assumed by the buyer should continue to be reflected on the seller's balance sheet, with appropriate disclosure that such properties and debt are subject to a sales contract. (Even nonrecourse debt assumed by the buyer should not be offset against the related property.)
- Subsequent payments on the debt assumed by the buyer become additional deposits and thereby reduce the seller's mortgage debt payable and increase the deposit liability account until a sale is recorded for accounting purposes.
- Depreciation should be continued.

AICPA *Statement of Position 78–4* indicates that since the property is, in substance, considered to be owned by the seller for accounting purposes, the occurrence of a legal sale that is accounted for under the deposit method should not cause the seller to terminate recording depreciation.

An example illustrating the application of the deposit method is set forth in Table 11.1.

Provision for Loss

Under the deposit method, no sale is recorded by the seller. However, if a loss is indicated under the terms of the transaction, it should be provided for and reflected as a valuation allowance. The net carrying value of the property, less the total of the debt assumed by the buyer and the nonrefundable deposits received by the seller should not exceed the fair value of the unrecorded note receivable based upon an appropriate current rate of interest.

If circumstances indicate that it is likely that the buyer will default and the property will revert to the seller, a provision for an additional loss may be required. Such circumstances may include deteriorating value of the property after the time of legal sale, but prior to the time of recording a sale for accounting purposes.

Nonrecourse Debt Exceeds Net Carrying Value

In some transactions that would fail the test for recording a sale solely as a result of inadequate buyer's investment, nonrecourse debt assumed by the buyer exceeds the net carrying value of the property (less nonrefundable deposits). In such cases, income may be assured to the extent of the excess if it is virtually assured—through management's clearly stated intention or otherwise—that the property will not revert to the seller. When such circumstances exist, the cost recovery method of accounting would be appropriate. Under that method, the property, the related nonrecourse mortgage debt, and the deposit should be removed from the balance sheet accounts and the transaction reported as a sale. Income would be recognized as earned only to the extent that the sum of the nonrecourse debt and nonrefundable deposits exceeds the net carrying value of the property.

Recording a Sale

Under the deposit method, a sale may not be recorded for accounting purposes until the conditions in the *Profit Recognition Accounting Guide* are met. As set forth in AICPA *Statement of Position 75–6,* the date from

Table 11.1.   Application of the Deposit Method

Assumptions		
1. Cost of land		$ 400,000

2. Terms of transaction	
Cash down payment (25% required for full profit recognition)	$ 10,000
First mortgage to seller (10% interest—5 year level amortization of principal)	490,000
Total sales price and sales value	$ 500,000

	Date of Sale	Year 1
3. Payments by buyer		
Cash down payment	$10,000	
First mortgage—		
Principal		$ 98,000
Interest		49,000
	$10,000	$147,000
Cumulative deposits	$10,000	$157,000

Results

Date of Sale.   The down payment by the buyer is insignificant compared to the sales value and recognition of the sale is deferred. The property and the existing first mortgage debt should continue to be recorded on the seller's financial statements. The $10,000 received should be recorded as a deposit liability.

End of Year 1.   Recognition of the sale is appropriate since the buyer's cash deposits result in a total down payment in excess of the 25 percent required. Interest received and credited to the deposit account can be included in the down payment and the sales value at the time a sale is recorded. The cash payments of $157,000 exceed 25 percent of $549,000 which is the total of the sales price of $500,000 increased by interest on the mortgage totaling $49,000. The seller can record the sale and the mortgage receivable of $392,000 from the buyer. A gain on the sale of $149,000, which includes the interest recorded in the first year, is appropriate assuming all other conditions for profit recognition have been met.

which the cumulative test would begin to apply would be delayed until the sale is recorded for accounting purposes. Therefore, for purposes of the down payment tests, interest received and credited to the deposit account can be included in the down payment and sales value at the time a sale is recorded.

Forfeiture of Deposit

If a buyer defaults and forfeits his nonrefundable deposit, the deposit liability is no longer required and may be credited to income. The circumstances underlying the default should, however, be carefully reviewed since such circumstances may indicate deteriorating value of the property. If so, it may be appropriate to treat the credit as a valuation reserve. These circumstances may require a provision for additional loss.

INSTALLMENT METHOD

When the substance of a real estate transaction indicates that a sale has occurred for accounting purposes, but collectibility of the total sales price cannot be reasonably estimated ·(such as when the buyer's investment is inadequate), the installment method may be appropriate. Circumstances, however, may indicate that the cost recovery method is required or is otherwise more appropriate. For example, when the deferred gross profit exceeds the net carrying value of the related receivable, profit may have been earned to the extent of such excess.

Accounting Procedures

The installment method apportions each principal collection between cost recovered and profit recognized in the same ratio as cost and profit are presumed to constitute sales value. Interest received on the related receivable is properly recorded as income when received.

In the application of the installment method, the *Profit Recognition Accounting Guide* stipulates in paragraph 37, however, that:

. . . caution should be exercised that the recorded asset amounts less deferred profit, if any, do not exceed the depreciated values had the property not been sold. It would be inappropriate to avoid charging losses in value to income by accomplishing a thinly financed "sale" under which the risk of losses in value continue to rest with the seller. Under these circumstances, the transaction is probably not in substance a sale.

Application of Installment Method When Debt is Assumed by the Buyer

In some sale transactions the buyer will assume an existing mortgage loan. If the seller has a contingent liability for such debt, the seller continues to have a risk of financial loss similar to the risk that would exist if the seller held a receivable from the buyer for that part of the proceeds. Therefore, under the installment method, as prescribed by AICPA *Statement of Position 78–4,* the profit to be recognized should be based on the cash collected as a percentage of the total sales value. This would include debt assumed by the buyer regardless of whether such debt is recourse or nonrecourse. An example illustrating an application of this principle is set forth in Table 11.2.

If the seller has no contingent liability for debt assumed by the buyer,

Table 11.2.   Application of the Installment Method

Assumptions	
Cash down payment (25% required for full profit recognition)	$ 150,000
Second mortgage (12% payable by buyer to seller—10 year	
amortization)	350,000
Total cash to be received by seller	500,000
First mortgage assumed by buyer—full recourse to seller (9%	
—20 year amortization)	500,000
Total sales price and sales value	$1,000,000
Cost	$ 600,000
Total Profit	$ 400,000

Accounting under the Installment Method

The down payment is inadequate. The installment method would permit initial profit recognition of $60,000 representing 40% ($400,000/$1,000,000) of $150,000.

Subsequent principal payments by the buyer on the first mortgage debt are treated as additional cash collections upon which profit would be recorded.

as may be the case when the buyer assumes a nonrecourse mortgage or obtains his own first mortgage borrowing, AICPA *Statement of Position 78–4* indicates that:

> For the purpose of applying the installment method, there should be no distinction between recourse and nonrecourse debt assumed by the buyer, because the seller may be motivated to honor the debt assumed by the buyer for various reasons, even though the seller is not contingently liable for the debt.

Wrap-Around or All-Inclusive Mortgage

In some sale transactions, the buyer will give the seller a wrap-around or all-inclusive mortgage which provides that the seller must continue payments on the first mortgage. According to AICPA *Statement of Position 78–4,* the profit to be recognized should be based on the principal cash collected as a percentage of total sales value, which would include the full amount of the wrap-around mortgage (not offset by the existing first mortgage), even if the first mortgage is nonrecourse.

Financial Statement Presentation

Under the installment method, at the time of sale the income statement would reflect the total sales value (from which the deferred gross profit would be deducted) and the total cost of sale. Deferred gross profit subsequently earned would be presented as a separate revenue item. In the balance sheet, deferred gross profit would be presented as a deduction from the related receivable. This method is illustrated in Table 11.3.

Change from Installment Method to Full Accrual Method

When developments subsequent to the adoption of the installment method show that collectibility of the sales price is reasonably assured, continued use of the installment method is no longer appropriate. If there were no other conditions that require deferral of profit recognition (such as the seller's continuing involvement with the property sold or a decline in the value of the property sold), it would be appropriate at that time to recog-

Table 11.3. Financial Statement Presentation Under Installment Method

The sale was recorded on December 31, 1979.

Income statement	1979	1980	1981
Sales	$1000		
Deferred profit	(342)		
Deferred profit recognized		$ 29	$ 31
Interest income		42	38
Revenues	658	71	69
Cost of sales	225		
Selling and administrative expense	300		
	525		
Income before income taxes	$ 133	$ 71	$ 69
Balance sheet			
Mortgage receivable	$ 720	$658	$592
Less deferred profit	(342)	(313)	(282)
	$ 378	$345	$310

The deferred profit in the income statement and the balance sheet could also be reflected parenthetically.

nize in income the profit attributable to the uncollected portion of the sales value.

Usually, the only circumstance which might provide a reasonable basis for estimating the collectibility of the remaining uncollected balance of the sales value would be collection (on a cumulative basis from the date the sale was first recorded on the installment basis for accounting purposes) of the aggregate amounts contemplated under the down payment and continuing investment requirements.

Discontinuing use of the installment method for reporting profit on a sale of real estate does not constitute a change in accounting principle. It is required as a result of changed conditions regarding the collectibility of the receivable. However, if discontinuing has a material effect on the seller's financial position or results of operations, the seller's financial statements should disclose the effect of, and the reason for, recognizing the profit in income on the uncollected portion of the sales value.

COST RECOVERY METHOD

When the substance of a real estate transaction indicates that a sale has occurred for accounting purposes, but that no profit should be recognized until costs are recouped, the cost recovery method must be used. This method would be required in situations such as the following:

- The receivable is subject to future subordination (page 70).
- The seller retains an interest in the property sold and the buyer has preferences (page 90).
- Uncertainty exists as to whether all or a portion of the cost will be recovered.
- There is uncertainty as to the amount of proceeds.

Furthermore, as a practical matter, the cost recovery method can always be used as an alternative to the installment method.

Accounting Procedures

Under the cost recovery method, no profit is recognized until cash collections (including principal and interest payments) and existing debt assumed by the buyer exceed the cost of the property sold. Cash collections in excess of cost should be recorded as revenue in the period of collection.

When applying the cost recovery method, the *Profit Recognition Accounting Guide* stipulates in paragraph 37 that:

> . . . caution should be exercised that the recorded asset amounts less deferred profit, if any, do not exceed the depreciated values had the property not been sold. It would be inappropriate to avoid charging losses in value to income by accomplishing a thinly financed "sale" under which the risk of losses in value continue to rest with the seller. Under these circumstances, the transaction is probably not in substance a sale.

An example illustrating the application of the cost recovery method is set forth in Table 11.4.

Financial Statement Presentation

Under the cost recovery method, the income statement at the time of sale would reflect the total sales value from which the deferred gross profit

Table 11.4.   Application of the Cost Recovery Method

Assumptions
1. Land is sold to a builder for development. The receivable from the buyer is payable only out of future development profits.
2. Composition of sales price:

Cash down payment	$ 250,000
Receivable from buyer, interest only for 6 years with balloon payment	400,000
	$ 650,000
3. Cost of property	$ 200,000

Accounting by the seller

A profit of $50,000 would be recorded at closing ($250,000 cash received less cost of $200,000). The collection of the $400,000 is contingent on future profits, if any. It should, therefore, not be recorded for accounting purposes until collected.

---

would be deducted, and the total cost of sale. Deferred gross profit, subsequently earned, would be presented as a separate item of revenue. The balance sheet would reflect the receivable from which the deferred gross profit would be deducted. This method is illustrated in Table 11.3. Principal collections would reduce the recorded receivable. Interest collections would increase the deferred profit on the balance sheet until such time as it is appropriate to record income. For an all-inclusive or wrap-around receivable held by the seller, interest collected may be recognized as income to the extent of interest expense on prior lien financing for which the seller remains responsible.

Some believe that the cost recovery method is not a method of recording a sale, and that the sale should not be reflected in the income statement and the receivable should not be reflected on the balance sheet. They believe that the accounting should be similar to the deposit method, except that collections of principal and interest should be reflected as a reduction of the carrying value of the property. This accounting treatment is also considered to be acceptable.

Change from Cost Recovery Method to Full Accrual Method

When conditions requiring or permitting the use of the cost recovery method would no longer exist, continued use of the cost recovery method is no longer appropriate. The change would be similar to the change from the installment method to the full accrual method discussed on page 138.

FINANCING METHOD

A real estate transaction may be, in substance, a financing arrangement rather than a sale. This frequently is the case where the seller has an obligation to repurchase the property (or can be compelled by the buyer to repurchase the property) at a price higher than the total amount of the payments received and to be received. In addition, the *Profit Recognition Accounting Guide* places an "option" to repurchase in the same class with an "obligation" to repurchase, thus prohibiting the recording of a sale when a seller has an "option" to repurchase property.

Accounting Procedures

Accounting procedures under the financing method should be similar to the accounting procedures under the deposit method with one exception. Under the financing method, the difference between (a) the total amount of all payments received and to be received, and (b) the repurchase price, is presumed to be interest expense. This should be accrued on the interest method over the period from the receipt of cash to the date of repurchase. As in the deposit method, cash received is reflected as a liability in the balance sheet. Thus at the date of repurchase, the full amount of the repurchase obligation should be recorded as a liability.

In the case of a repurchase option, if the surrounding facts and circumstances at the time of the sale transaction indicate a presumption or a likelihood that the seller will exercise his option, interest should be accrued in the same manner as if there were an obligation to repurchase. This presumption could result from the value of property, the property being an integral part of development, or management's intention. If such a presumption does not exist at the time of the sale transaction, interest should not be accrued and the deposit method is believed to be appropriate.

LEASE METHOD

A real estate transaction may be, in substance, a lease rather than a sale. Accounting procedures under the lease method should be similar to the deposit method as described on page 132 with the exception of the following:

- Payments received and to be received, which are in substance deferred rental income, should be amortized to income over the presumed lease period. This amortization to income should not exceed the cash paid to the seller.
- Cash paid out by the seller as a guarantee of support of operations should be expensed as paid.

Loan to Buyer

The seller may agree to make loans to the buyer in support of operations, such as when cash flow does not equal a predetermined amount or is negative. In such a situation, deferred rental income to be amortized to income should be reduced by all the loans made or reasonably anticipated to be made to the buyer, thus reducing the periodic income to be recognized. Where the loans made or anticipated to be made exceed deferred rental income, a loss provision may be required if the collectibility of the loan is questionable.

Seller Has Option or Obligation to Repurchase

The seller may have an option or an obligation to repurchase the property at an amount lower than the total amount received or to be received. Such a transaction may be, in substance, part lease and part financing. In this situation, the lease method may be appropriate, but only the difference between the repurchase price and the total amount to be received on the sale should be considered deferred rental income to be amortized, subject to the limitation described in the example in Table 11.5 which illustrates the application of the lease method. Alternatively, it would also be appropriate to charge interest expense at an appropriate amount as it relates to the repurchase obligation with a corresponding increase in rental income. The repurchase price should be considered an obligation payable.

PROFIT SHARING (OR CO-VENTURE) METHOD

A real estate transaction may be, in substance, a profit sharing arrangement rather than a sale. For example, a sale of real estate to a limited

Table 11.5. Application of Lease Method

Assumptions

  Total sale price and cash payment—$1,000,000
  Seller's carrying value—$900,000
  Seller has option to repurchase in 10 years at a price of $600,000

Result

  As a result of the option to repurchase, no sale or profit may be recorded at the time of sale. The cash payment of $1,000,000 represents a deposit. Of this amount, $400,000 is presumed to be rental income that should be amortized to income in the amount of $40,000 annually and $600,000 represents the amount payable to exercise the repurchase option.

Limitation

  Amortization of deferred rental income in this manner could, in some cases, result in an inherent loss as a result of a decision not to exercise an option to repurchase if the total of the repurchase price would be less than the carrying value of the property at the date of repurchase. In this case, only a portion of the income should be reflected.

  In this example, if the carrying value of the property sold was being depreciated over 45 years ($20,000 per year), at the end of the 10th year the carrying value would be $700,000 as compared to a repurchase price of $600,000. The sales proceeds to be recorded would be less than the carrying value of the property and, therefore, a loss of $100,000 would result. Thus, in this situation, deferred income to be amortized would be limited to $300,000 ($1,000,000 less $700,000) or $30,000 per year.

---

partnership in which the seller is a general partner or has similar characteristics is often a profit sharing arrangement. If the transaction does not meet the test for recording a sale, it usually would be accounted for under the profit sharing method.

This accounting method should also be followed when it is clear that the buyer is acting merely as an agent for the seller. In these situations, giving consideration to the seller's continued involvement, the seller would be required to account for the operations of the property through its income statement as if the seller continued to own the properties.

Accounting Procedures

An appropriate method of accounting under the profit sharing or coventure method would be:

- Property should be transferred to an investment account, which should be amortized over the life of the improvements. Alternatively, the property could remain as an asset and be depreciated over its useful life;
- Any related mortgage debt assumed by the buyer should continue to be reflected on the seller's balance sheet;
- Notes receivable arising from the transaction should not be recorded;
- Results of operations of the property (before depreciation and before payments to the seller) should be reflected on the seller's income statement and should include adjustments for the following:
  - (a) Cash paid out from operations to the other investors of the buyer—such as a distribution of profits or operating cash flow—should be reflected as an additional expense.
  - (b) Cash paid in by the other investors of the buyer in support of operations should be reflected as a reduction of expense. Income from operations should be added to the investment account. Losses from operations should be reflected as a reduction of the investment account. The results may be reflected as "gross" or "net" in the income statement. If reflected as "net," the footnotes should include information on the property's revenues and expenses;
- Cash paid out by the seller in support of operations (or as a loan for operations) should be added to the investment account since, as described above, losses from operations have already been reflected in the seller's income statement;
- Cash collected by the seller (such as down payment, principal and interest, management fees and distributions from operations) from the buyer should be reflected as a reduction of the investment account.

There also may be other appropriate methods of application of the profit sharing or co-venture method but, in all such methods, the general concept of requiring the seller to reflect the operations of the property through its income statement should be followed.

PART THREE

ACCOUNTING FOR INVESTMENTS IN REAL ESTATE VENTURES

Chapter 12

Introduction and
Accounting Background

Venture arrangements can be traced back to the days when merchants and investors banded together to share the risks and rewards of seafaring trading expeditions. In this country, venture arrangements have been widely used for many years in the construction, mining, and oil and gas industries, and, more recently, for real estate developments. Real estate ventures generally are entered into by two or more venturers to pool technology, development capabilities and financial resources.

VENTURE CHARACTERISTICS

A real estate venture typically has the following characteristics:

- The entity is owned and operated by a small group of investors as a separate business or project for their mutual benefit;
- Each investor participates, directly or indirectly, in overall management. Arrangements are usually made at formation through a joint venture or partnership agreement; and
- Each of the investors can exercise significant influence over the venture's operations.

One investor ordinarily does not have control by direct or indirect ownership of a majority voting interest. Otherwise, the venture is likely to be a subsidiary of the controlling investor.

VENTURE PARTICIPANTS

The parties normally found in a real estate venture take four roles: *landowner, investor, developer,* and *lender.* Typically, more than one of these roles are combined in one venture. Participation by a venturer often includes some of these activities:

Landowner (usually relatively inactive unless filling two roles):

- Contributes land for venture interest;
- Contributes land for venture interest and preferred cash flow;
- Sells land for note subordinated to other lenders and for joint venture interest.

Investor (other than landowner—usually relatively inactive):

- Invests cash for venture interest:
    May or may not get preferred return;
    May get preference on tax attributes.

Developer (usually has operational control within predetermined constraints):

- Contributes services for venture interest;
- Sells services and gets venture interest for management without cash involvement;
- Acts as general partner in limited partnership;
- May guarantee cash flow.

Lender (usually relatively inactive):

- Lends development funds and receives venture interest;
- Lends funds and makes equity investment in venture.

A party entering a real estate venture may have an interest in:

  (1) the venture equity in net assets and future profits and losses;
  (2) only future profits and losses; or
  (3) only future profits.

LEGAL FORM OF VENTURE

Real estate ventures are organized as corporate entities or, more frequently, as partnerships. Limited partnerships are often used because of the advantages of limited liability.

Basic definitions of the most common legal forms are:

Corporate Joint Venture. A corporation owned and operated by a small group of investors as a separate and specific business or project for the mutual benefit of members of the group. By incorporating, the investors avail themselves of the legal protection provided by the corporate veil and thereby limit their exposure. The ownership of a corporate joint venture seldom changes and its stock is usually not traded publicly.

General Partnership. An association in which each partner has unlimited liability.

Limited Partnership. An association in which one or more general partners have unlimited liability, and one or more partners have limited liability. Typically, a limited partnership is managed by the general partner(s) subject to limitations imposed by a partnership agreement, while the limited partners are not involved in day-to-day operations.

Undivided Interest. An ownership arrangement in which two or more parties jointly own property (title is held individually to the extent of each party's interest) and are severally liable for indebtedness of their respective interests. This form of arrangement has not been widely used in real estate ventures.

Regardless of the legal form, the accounting principles should be the same for recognition of profits and losses, although financial statement presentation may vary.

ACCOUNTING BACKGROUND

Accounting practices in the real estate industry in general and, more specifically, accounting for investments in real estate ventures have varied, resulting in a lack of comparability and, in some cases, comprehension. The exercise of much judgment, therefore, was required in deciding upon appropriate and meaningful accounting. In recent years, the following relevant pronouncements have been issued.

Accounting Principles Board Opinion No. 18—1971

Because of the general variation in accounting for investments, in March 1971, the Accounting Principles Board (APB) issued *Opinion No. 18* on the equity method of accounting for investments in common stock. This opinion may also be considered applicable to investments in unincorporated ventures, including partnerships, because of a November 1971 interpretation of the AICPA.

AICPA Accounting Guide: Accounting for Profit Recognition on Sales of Real Estate—1973

In 1973, the AICPA issued the *Profit Recognition Accounting Guide* which discusses the timing of profit recognition on real estate sales, particularly with respect to the buyer's investment in the property and the continuing involvement of the seller with the property sold. This aspect is particularly important for accounting for transactions between the investors and the venture as discussed in this book. In addition, this guide discusses the application of APB *Opinion No. 18* to sales of real estate to a buyer in which the seller holds or acquires an equity interest. The guide sets forth broad principles of accounting but, because of the complexities of real estate sales, its application continues to present new and challenging real estate accounting problems.

Investor Accounting for Real Estate Joint Ventures

Because of the lack of authoritative literature on investor accounting for real estate ventures, in 1975 Price Waterhouse & Co. published a booklet, *Investor Accounting for Real Estate Joint Ventures*. It, for the first time, brought together and discussed many of the various special problems investors encounter in practice—problems that are covered in this book.

AICPA Statement of Position 78-9—1978

The AICPA recognized the continuing diverse practices and in December 1978 issued *Statement of Position* (SOP) *78-9,* "Accounting for Investments in Real Estate Ventures." While this SOP does not constitute standards that are enforceable under the AICPA's Code of Professional Ethics, it does represent the conclusions of at least a majority of the Accounting Standards Executive Committee which is the senior technical body authorized to speak for the AICPA in the areas of financial accounting and reporting. More importantly, it draws upon authoritative accounting literature and applies it to investments in real estate ventures.

Specifically, many of the requirements of *Accounting Principles Board Opinion No. 18* and the related AICPA accounting interpretation issued in November 1971 are included in the SOP. The SOP, based in large part on the aforementioned Price Waterhouse booklet, was issued to narrow the range of alternative practices used in real estate venture accounting and to establish uniformity within the industry.

The AICPA recommended that adjustments resulting from a change in accounting method to comply with recommendations in the SOP should be applied retroactively, if material. Financial statements presented for prior periods that were affected should be restated for as many periods as practicable in order to give retroactive effect to such adjustments and to changes in presentation.

It should be pointed out that *Financial Accounting Standards Board Interpretation No. 20,* "Reporting Accounting Changes Under AICPA Statements of Position," issued as an interpretation of *APB Opinion No. 20,* concluded that an enterprise making a change in accounting principle to conform with the recommendations of an AICPA Statement of Position ". . . shall report the change as specified in the statement."

Chapter 13

Accounting for Results of Operations of Ventures

Before determining the appropriate accounting for venture income, it is important to distinguish between situations where the investor controls the venture and those where it does not. The legal form of the entity is usually not a significant factor in determining appropriate accounting for results of operations. Control can be defined as follows:

Corporations. The usual condition for control is ownership of a majority interest (over 50 percent) in the outstanding voting stock. The power to control may also exist with a smaller percentage of voting interests, such as by contract, agreement with venture partners or court decree.

General Partnerships. Control, here, is generally the same as with a corporation. However, if voting interests are not clearly indicated, ownership of a majority (over 50 percent) of the financial interests in profits or losses usually indicates control. On the other hand, majority ownership may not constitute control if major decisions, such as the acquisition, sale, or refinancing of principal partnership assets, must be approved by one or more of the other partners.

Limited Partnerships. The rights and obligations of general partners are different from those of limited partners. A general partner may be in control regardless of his ownership or financial interest when the substance of the partnership arrangement or other agreements provide for his control. This may be the case when the general partner decides on major operating and financial policies of the partnership and cannot be removed.

If such conditions do not exist, a limited partner may be in control if it holds over 50 percent of the total partnership interest.

Undivided Interests. Control is generally not present because each investor owns an undivided interest in each venture asset and is liable for its share of each liability. If this is not the case, these arrangements should be treated as a general partnership.

INVESTOR ACCOUNTING FOR INCOME AND LOSSES

In order to determine the appropriate method of accounting for income and losses, it must first be determined whether or not the investor controls the venture.

Controlling Investor—Consolidate

A controlling investor should account for its income and losses under the principles of accounting that apply to investments in subsidiaries. This usually requires consolidation of the venture's operations, with appropriate recognition of minority interests.

Regarding corporate entities, paragraph 1 of *Accounting Research Bulletin No. 51* states:

> There is a presumption that consolidated statements are more meaningful than separate statements and that they are usually necessary for a fair presentation when one of the companies in the group directly or indirectly has a controlling financial interest in the other companies.

The application of consolidation principles to investments in partnerships and other unincorporated ventures should not be different from those applicable to corporations. Nonetheless, in each case, the investor must carefully analyze the provisions of the agreement, and the facts and circumstances surrounding the investor's interests to determine if control is present.

If the venture is operating in a foreign country where realization of venture earnings by the investor is subject to major uncertainties—such as may be the case where there are exchange restrictions, governmental controls and substantial political, economic, or social disruptions or uncertainties—it is inappropriate to consolidate these operations or recognize the investor's share of the earnings until they are remitted as dividends or distributions.

Noncontrolling Investor—Equity Method

A noncontrolling investor should account for its share of income and losses in real estate ventures by using the equity method. *Accounting Principles Board Opinion No. 18* concluded in paragraph 16 that:

> . . . investors should account for investments in common stock of corporate joint ventures by the equity method. . . .

Usually, in order to apply the equity method, the investment must be 20 percent. But, as described in the Opinion, this percentage does not apply to joint ventures. Therefore, as a general rule, investors should account for all unincorporated joint venture interests (including general and limited partnership interests) by using the equity method.

The cost method, however, is appropriate in certain situations such as (a) for ventures engaged in foreign operations where realization is subject to major uncertainties and (b) for limited partnerships where the investor's interest is so insignificant that the limited partner has virtually no influence over operating and financial policies. (An example would be a very minor interest in a public limited partnership.) As with all investments, the owner should assess the recoverability and make appropriate write-downs where necessary. Although not common in the real estate industry, the proportionate share method may be appropriate where stringent criteria are met for "undivided interests." (See page 189.)

Equity Method Versus Cost Method

Under the equity method, the initial investment is recorded by the investor at cost. Thereafter, the carrying amount is increased by the investor's share of current earnings and decreased by the investor's share of current losses or distributions.

Under the cost method, the initial investment is recorded by the investor at cost. Thereafter, income is recognized only when distributions are received by the investor from earnings subsequent to the acquisition or when the investor sells its interest in the venture.

Table 13.1. Equity Method Versus Cost Method

Assumptions
1. Investor *A* contributes cash of $300,000 for a 30% interest in a venture at the formation of the venture, which will own and operate an office building.
2. The earnings and cash distributions of the venture for the first two years are as follows:

Year	Earnings	Distributions
1	$ 60,000	–
2	$100,000	$50,000

Accounting by the investor

Year	Investment at beginning of year	Investor's share of earnings of venture	Cash received	Investment at end of year
Cost method:				
1	$300,000	–	–	$300,000
2	300,000	–	$15,000	300,000
Total income (before income taxes) years 1–2			$15,000	
Equity method:				
1	$300,000	$18,000	–	$318,000
2	318,000	30,000	($15,000)	333,000
Total income (before income taxes) years 1–2		$48,000		

The effect of applying the equity method rather than the cost method is illustrated in Table 13.1.

Accounting Principles Used by the Venture

For the purpose of investor accounting, the results of operations and the financial position of a venture must be determined in accordance with generally accepted accounting principles.

It is not uncommon for real estate ventures to utilize accounting practices expressly for other purposes, such as the preparation of tax basis data for investors. These practices may include expensing certain costs for tax purposes that are usually capitalized for books. In such cases, an investor must make adjustments to eliminate the effect of any material variances from generally accepted accounting principles. Each adjustment, however, must be carefully considered as it would be inappropriate to capitalize costs at the investor level when it would be inappropriate, under generally accepted accounting principles, at the venture level. Of course, any tax timing difference should be accounted for by the investor in accordance with *Accounting Principles Board Opinion No. 11,* "Accounting for Income Taxes."

An example illustrating the above is set forth in Table 13.2.

Varying Profit Participations
for Accounting Purposes

In accounting for investments in real estate ventures, it is important to recognize that some venture agreements may designate different allocations among the venturers of profits and losses, distributions of cash from operations, and distribution of cash proceeds on liquidation. Also, one or more of the allocation arrangements may change with the lapse of time or the occurrence of specified events.

In these circumstances, accounting for an investor's equity in venture earnings must be carefully considered and particular attention must be paid to the possibility that the allocation of profits and losses as specified in the venture agreement may not reflect the economic substance of the transaction. It is not appropriate to use the specified profit and loss allocation ratios to determine an investor's equity in venture earnings when the allocation of cash distributions is determined on a basis other than the profit and loss allocation ratios or when, after reflecting all previous profits and losses, cash distributions in liquidation are not based on the balances in the venturers' capital accounts.

Equity in venture earnings must be determined on a realistic pretax income basis. For example, to determine the share of the venture's pretax income, consideration should be given to how any reported increase in net assets will ultimately affect cash payments to the investor, either over the life of the venture or in liquidation. The difference between the equity in

Table 13.2.   Reporting by Investors Under Generally Accepted Accounting Practices

Assumptions
1. Investors X, Y, and Z each own a ⅓ interest in a venture and account for their investment under the equity method.
2. Venture XYZ sold property with a carrying value of $1,000,000 to an independent third party for $1,600,000. The sale was recorded by the venture on the installment method for both book and tax purposes.
3. The sale qualifies for full profit recognition under the *Profit Recognition Accounting Guide.*
4. Proceeds from the sale were collected and the pro rata gain was reported as follows:

Year	Proceeds	Gain
1	$ 480,000	$180,000
2	280,000	105,000
3	280,000	105,000
4	280,000	105,000
5	280,000	105,000
	$1,600,000	$600,000

Venture XYZ had no other transactions in years 1 through 5.
5. The tax effects of the transaction have been ignored for purposes of this illustration.

Accounting by the Investor
Under generally accepted accounting principles, it is appropriate for Venture XYZ to recognize the entire gain ($600,000) in Year 1, but because the venture reports to its investors on a tax basis of accounting, the venture has recorded the transaction using the installment basis. For the investors to report under generally accepted accounting principles, adjustments to the reported tax basis are required:

Year	Venture XYZ income	Adjustments	As adjusted	One-third equity interest
1	$180,000	$420,000	$600,000	$200,000
2	105,000	(105,000)	–	–
3	105,000	(105,000)	–	–
4	105,000	(105,000)	–	–
5	105,000	(105,000)	–	–
	$600,000	-0-	$600,000	$200,000

As illustrated, Investors X, Y, and Z would record their one-third interest ($200,000) in the net income of Venture XYZ in Year 1.

159

pretax income thus determined and that reported for tax purposes is a timing difference for which tax allocation principles must be followed. An example illustrating the above is set forth in Table 13.3.

SPECIAL ACCOUNTING PROBLEMS RELATED
TO RECOGNITION OF LOSSES

Investors should record their shares of venture losses as determined in accordance with generally accepted accounting principles. In some real estate ventures, losses incurred may not be cash losses but bookkeeping losses resulting from depreciation. In addition, there are many who believe that consideration should be given to unrealized increases in the fair value of the venturers' assets before recording the investor's share of losses. Generally accepted accounting principles, however, do not permit an investor to use a different accounting principle for a partial ownership interest than that which it would be required to use if it had full ownership. The exception to the rule follows.

Recognition of Losses in Excess
of an Investor's Investment

An investor should recognize its share of venture losses—even though its investment (including loans and advances) is reduced to zero by continuing to apply the equity method—when it is committed to absorbing these losses because of its stated or implied guarantee of venture obligations or financial support of operations. Examples of these circumstances are as follows:

- Legal obligations (for example, as guarantor or general partner);
- Quasi-legal obligations, based on such factors as business reputation, intercompany relationships, and credit standing;
- A presumption supported by past performance that the investor would make good venture obligations; and/or
- Public statements that the investor intends to support venture operations.

In addition to the above, an investor—although not liable or otherwise committed to provide additional financial support—should provide for

Table 13.3. Allocation of Income and Losses

Assumptions
1. Investors *A, B, C,* and *D* form a partnership for the development and operation of an office building. Investments by each of the partners upon formation were as follows: Investor *A* contributed land having a fair value and cost basis of $1,000,000; Investors *B, C,* and *D* each contributed $1,000,000 in cash.
2. Investor *A* is to develop and operate the property.
3. The partnership agreement stipulates that earnings and losses from the venture are to be allocated as follows: Investors *B, C,* and *D* share equally in all operating losses with none allocated to Investor *A;* operating profits and all cash flows are to be allocated in proportion to their contributions (25%). In addition, proceeds to be received upon liquidation of the operating properties are also to be allocated in proportion to the contributions (25%).
4. Results of operations for the partnership and their allocations to the respective partners for the first three years are:

| | | Allocation to Partners | |
Year	Income (loss)	A	B, C, D
1	($400,000)	$ —	($400,000)
2	(100,000)	—	(100,000)
3	150,000	37,500	112,500

Accounting by the Investors

The above table illustrates the allocations of partnership income (losses) pursuant to the terms of the partnership agreement. However, the economic reality of the arrangement is that each partner will ultimately share equally in the economic gain or loss resulting from operations and/or liquidation of the property. Accordingly, operating profits and losses should be recorded proportionately by the investors as follows:

Year		Investor's equity in income (losses)
1	25% × ($400,000)	($100,000)
2	25% × ($100,000)	($ 25,000)
3	25% × $150,000	$ 37,500

losses in excess of investment when the imminent return to profitable operations by the venture appears to be assured. For example, a material nonrecurring loss of an isolated nature may reduce an investment below zero although the underlying profitable pattern of an investee is unimpaired.

When the investor records losses in excess of its investment (including loans and advances), the resulting negative balance in the investment account should be reflected as a liability on the investor's financial statements.

When venture losses in excess of investment are not recognized and the venture subsequently reports income, the investor should resume recognition of its share of venture earnings only after its share of subsequent net income equals that share of net losses that it had not previously recognized during the period in which the equity method was suspended. The general principle of recognizing losses in excess of investment is illustrated in Table 13.4.

Recognition of Losses in Excess of Investor's Proportionate Share

Situations can arise in which one or more investors may not be able to bear their share of venture losses. If cash losses are incurred and an investor cannot bear its share of the losses, the remaining investors should record proportionate shares of the entire amount of venture losses. Subsequent earnings of the venture should be recorded by those other investors to the extent that such earnings equal the previously recorded excess losses. Recognition of the loss by the other venturers, however, does not exempt a financially incapable investor from recording its allocable share unless relieved from the obligation by agreement or by law. Judgment must be exercised over whether an investor is unable to bear its share of losses, but the probability should be based on the provisions of *Financial Accounting Standards No. 5*, "Accounting for Contingencies." An example to illustrate the above is set forth in Table 13.5.

Loss in Value of Investment

Statement of Position 78–9 has adopted a position comparable to that in paragraph 19 of *Accounting Principles Board Opinion No. 18* that indi-

Table 13.4.   Recognition of Losses in Excess of Investment

Assumptions
1. Investor *A* invests $200,000 for a 25% interest in a venture formed to own and operate an apartment building.
2. Additional financing for the venture is negotiated with an independent lender for $3,500,000, of which $3,000,000 is secured by a nonrecourse first mortgage on the property and $500,000 is secured by a second mortgage that is guaranteed by the investors.
3. Losses were reported by the venture during its first three years of operations as follows: Year 1—$450,000; Year 2—$250,000 and Year 3—$200,000.

Accounting by the Investor

Under the equity method, Investor *A*'s investment account at the end of Year 2 would be $25,000, determined as follows:

Initial capital contribution	$200,000
Equity in losses of venture for:	
Year 1 ($450,000 × 25%)	(112,500)
Year 2 ($250,000 × 25%)	(62,500)
Balance at end of Year 2	$ 25,000

Since Investor *A* is obligated as a guarantor on the $500,000 loan, he is required to continue recording his share of venture losses. This will result in a negative balance in the investment account:

Balance at end of Year 2 (see above)	$25,000
Equity in loss of venture for Year 3	
($200,000 × 25%)	(50,000)
Balance at end of Year 3	($25,000)

The negative balance ($25,000) in the investment account should be reflected as a liability in Investor *A*'s balance sheet.

Table 13.5.   Recognition of Losses in Excess of Proportionate Share

---

Assumptions
1. Investors *A, B, C,* and *D* each own a 25% interest in Venture XYZ—a general partnership. They share profits and losses according to their ownership percentages.
2. Each investor is obliged to fund future losses. For simplicity, assume that noncash charges are equal to principal payments on the mortgage.
3. Venture XYZ incurs an operating loss of $300,000.
4. Evidence exists that it is at least probable that Investor *D* cannot provide his $75,000 share of the loss (25% of $300,000).

Accounting by the Investor
Investors *A, B,* and *C* are each required to record equity in Venture XYZ losses as follows:

Allocable share of total loss—25% × $300,000	$ 75,000
Allocable share of Investor *D*'s loss—33⅓% × $75,000	25,000
Total loss to be recorded by Investors *A, B,* and *C*	$100,000

At the same time, Investor *D* must also record his share of the loss ($75,000).
In future periods, assuming Venture XYZ reports net income, Investors *A, B,* and *C* should record an additional share in the income equal to the previously recorded losses in excess of their allocable share.

---

cates that a loss in value of an investment (including loans and advances), other than a temporary decline, should be recognized under the accounting principles that apply to a loss in value of other long-term assets. Such a loss in value may be indicated, for example, by a decision of the other investors to discontinue providing support to the venture.

Inasmuch as the financial statements of the venture must be prepared in accordance with, or adjusted to, generally accepted accounting principles, such independent write-downs are uncommon. However, a write-down would be appropriate if the estimated net realizable value of an investment held for sale is determined to be less than its carrying value.

A write-down below equity in net assets is actually a reserve for losses, which may be fully or partially reversed when the reserve is clearly no longer required.

Chapter 14

Accounting for Transactions with a Real Estate Venture

Accounting Principles Board Opinion No. 18 provides that in applying the equity method, intercompany profits should be eliminated by the investor until realized by the investee as if the venture were consolidated. An AICPA Accounting Interpretation issued in November 1971 clarified this by stating that intercompany profit should be eliminated by the investor only to the extent of its ownership interest in the venture. Complete elimination of the intercompany profit is required by the investor, however, when it controls the venture or enters into a transaction with the venture which is not at "arm's length." The intercompany profit elimination is required until profit is realized by venture transactions with outside parties.

The *Profit Recognition Accounting Guide* also sets out similar rules in Paragraph 58:

> A sale of property in which the seller holds or acquires an equity interest in the buyer should result in recognizing only the part of the profit proportionate to the outside interest in the buyer. No profit should be recognized if the seller controls the buyer . . . until realized from transactions with outside parties through sale or operations of the property.

Intercompany losses usually should not be eliminated. They most likely represent a permanent loss in value of the asset sold because the transactions generally are objective evidence of the loss.

If an investor reports profit on a transaction with a venture in a period different from that in which a gain is reported for tax purposes, deferred income taxes should be provided on the timing difference in accordance with *Accounting Principles Board Opinion No. 11,* "Accounting for Income Taxes."

The next sections will discuss, in detail, the elimination of interentity profits for the following types of transactions:

Capital contributions to the venture;

Interest income on loans and advances to the venture;

Sales of real estate to the venture;

Sales of services to the venture; or

Venture sales of real estate or services to an investor.

CAPITAL CONTRIBUTIONS

Capital contributed to real estate ventures by investors usually takes one of the following forms:

Cash contributions;

Contribution of real estate;

Contribution of services or intangibles.

Accounting aspects for each are discussed in the following sections.

Cash Contributions

There are no accounting problems when all venturers contribute cash at the formation of the venture in proportion to each of their interests. The investor should record its investment in the venture based on the cash contributed.

Contribution of Real Estate

As set forth in *Statement of Position 78–9,* an investor contributing real estate as its capital contribution to a venture should record its investment in the venture at the investor's carrying value. This usually is defined as cost less related depreciation and valuation allowances. Under this method, the investor is precluded from recognizing any profit on the transaction until the earnings process is completed—which occurs when the property is sold to a third party. Profit recognition is permitted, however, in those rare circumstances when the contributing partner concurrently withdraws cash (or other hard assets) for the real estate contributed and is not obliged to reinvest such funds. Profit recognition on such sales would be subject to the criteria set forth elsewhere in this book.

The author believes that the guidelines on contribution of real estate that are described in SOP 78–9 are too stringent, unduly conservative, and inconsistent with the accounting criteria established for investor sales of real estate to a venture. In accounting for sales of real estate, a noncontrolling investor may recognize profit in many instances on a sale to a venture to the extent of other investors' proportionate interests in the venture. The criteria to be met in accounting for sales transactions are not so restrictive that they require total withdrawal of cash or hard assets before profit may be recognized.

There seems little difference, in the author's view, between an investor's contribution of real estate to a venture or a sale to a venture. Logically then, the accounting rules for profit recognition on the respective transactions should be comparable. However, the position expressed in SOP 78–9 clearly distinguishes between these transactions, and precludes the investor from recognizing any profit on a contribution of real estate.

Losses on the contribution of real estate to a joint venture should be recognized in full because such transactions, generally, are objective evidence of a permanent loss of value of the real estate.

Contribution of Services or Intangibles

The AICPA retained the above viewpoint in SOP 78–9 when considering accounting for contributions of services or intangibles to a venture. It maintained that the investor's cost is the only appropriate measure for recording contributions of services or intangibles to a venture. This, in effect, results in deferral of any profit recognition until it is realized in venture transactions with third parties.

INVESTOR ACCOUNTING FOR INTEREST INCOME ON LOANS AND ADVANCES TO A VENTURE

In some ventures, one of the investors lends funds for real estate development or other purposes. In other ventures, investors may be called upon to lend funds to sustain operations for a temporary period of time. These loans are typically in the form of interest-bearing notes. The appropriate method of accounting for interest received by the investor depends on a number of factors as outlined below.

Substance of Loan is a Capital Contribution

Some investor contributions to real estate ventures, while taking the form of interest-bearing loans and advances, may, in substance, constitute additional contributed capital. That is because there is a lack of objective evidence to differentiate between the role of an independent lender and investor. In such cases, interest accruing to the investor on monies deemed to represent contributed capital should be viewed as distributions for accounting purposes. In other words, such "interest" should be treated by the investor as a return on equity capital and recorded as a reduction in the investment account versus the interest income. An example illustrating the application of the foregoing concept is set forth in Table 14.1.

Substance of Loan is Not a Capital Contribution

When accounting for the interest income of a lender/investor, there are two separate elements of this income:

- The portion applicable to the equity interest of the lender/investor; and
- The portion applicable to the equity interest of the other investors.

The accounting for each portion is described below.

Portion Applicable to Equity Interest of the Lender/Investor. This portion of interest income of the investor should be deferred until the related interest expense is charged to operations by the venture. At such time, under the equity method, this portion of the interest income of the venturer and the expense of the venture would offset.

Portion Applicable to Equity Interest of Other Investors. This portion of interest income of the investor may be recognized if the loan is on the

Table 14.1.   Substance of Loan is a Capital Contribution

Assumptions
  Investors *A, B,* and *C* each invest $1,000,000 for a one-third interest in a
  real estate venture, and by agreement each lend $2,000,000 to the venture
  with interest payable at 10%.

Accounting by the Investor
  In this situation, the substance of the loans is viewed as additional capital
contributions by the partners. Consequently, interest earned on the $2,000,000
should be recorded as reductions in the investment account comparable to the
accounting treatment afforded distributions. If the venture expenses interest,
such expense should be eliminated in calculating the investor's share of the
results of operations of the venture.

---

same basis and terms as that of an independent lender. The lender/
investor's risks may, however, be substantially different from those of an
independent lender, requiring full deferral of the portion of the interest income that is applicable to the other investors until confirmed by venture
transactions with third parties or the interest expense is charged to operations by the venture, when any one of the following are present:

- Collectibility is in doubt such as may be the case where there is lack
  of (a) adequate collateral or (b) other conditions normally required
  by an independent lender;
- Circumstances exist where the investor's risks exceed his investments, loans, and advances (unless the other venturers have a sufficient capital investment in the venture so that they may reasonably
  be expected to bear their share of the risks of ownership); or
- Additional continuing involvement exists as outlined for sales of real
  estate. (See page 76.)

The above principles can be illustrated in the following examples.

1. Investors *A, B,* and *C* are all investors in a corporate joint venture.
   Each invests $1,000,000 for a one-third interest and, in addition, *A*
   lends $5,000,000 and *B* and *C* each lend $2,000,000 to the venture.
   In this case, *A* could record interest income to the extent of two
   thirds of the income on the additional $3,000,000.

2. Investors *A, B,* and *C* form a real estate venture in which each has a one-third equity ownership. Investor *A,* a passive investor, loans $1,000,000 to the venture with interest at ten percent. The loan is fully secured and Investors *B* and *C* have contributed sufficient capital to bear their share of venture losses. In this instance, Investor *A* may recognize the entire interest income provided that, in recording its equity in venture income, the related interest cost was expensed by the venture. If, on the other hand, the venture capitalized or otherwise deferred the interest expense, Investor *A* must defer recognition of one third of the interest income until the related interest expense is charged to operations by the venture.

The AICPA position in *Statement of Position 78–9* is similar to the preceding when the lender/investor expenses interest on its own construction and development projects. However, a position was not taken on a lender/investor that capitalizes interest pending conclusion of the Financial Accounting Standards Board project on Accounting for Interest Costs.

SALES OF REAL ESTATE TO THE VENTURE

When an investor sells real estate to the venture, the investor may not recognize profit if it controls the venture. If the investor does not control the venture, it may recognize profit to the extent of other investors' proportionate interests in the venture if all necessary requirements for profit recognition are satisfied. The portion of the profit applicable to the investor's equity interest should be deferred until such costs are charged to operations by the venture. This principle is illustrated in Table 14.2.

Profit recognition on sales of real estate is, generally, covered in Part II of this book. Stringent requirements for profit recognition include (1) minimum cash down payments ranging from five percent to 25 percent of sales value depending on the type of property involved, (2) annual amortization of the resulting receivable over an appropriate period, and (3) deferral of all or part of the profit under certain circumstances, including those in which the seller continues to be involved with the property.

For example, continuing involvement by the seller requiring deferral of all or a portion of the profit may exist in any of the following situations, when the seller:

Table 14.2.   Sales of Real Estate to a Venture

Assumptions
  1. Investor *A* sells land with an original cost of $80,000 to a 25%-owned joint venture (general partnership) for $120,000.
  2. The venture is in the development stage and has no income or losses.
  3. There is no continuing involvement of Investor *A* or other conditions requiring deferral of profit.

Accounting by the Investor
  A's income for the year includes gain on the sale as follows:

Selling price	$120,000
Cost of sales	80,000
Gross profit	40,000
Less deferred profit of 25%	10,000
Gain on sale	$ 30,000

Since *A*'s venture interest is 25%, *A* has made a sale to itself to that extent and a sale to its joint venture partners to the extent of 75%. Therefore, *A* should defer 25% of the profit on the sale and recognize it when the land is sold to a third party. Investor *A*, therefore, must reduce its gain of $40,000 by $10,000 (25% × $40,000 = $10,000).

- Will be required to support the property or related obligations to an extent greater than his proportionate interest;
- Has granted preferences as to profits or cash flow to the other investors;
- Is a general partner in a limited partnership holding an operating property and holds a significant receivable related to the property;
- Is required to support operations (such as guarantees and leaseback arrangements);
- Is otherwise presumed to be obligated to support operations (such as where the investor is a general partner in a limited partnership holding an operating property);
- Is responsible for managing, developing or constructing improvements on the property;
- Has an option or obligation to repurchase the property; or
- Is required to arrange or provide financing for the project.

This chapter deals with special problems unique to investors in joint ventures. In any sale of real estate, particular attention should be given to all of the requirements for profit recognition.

SALES OF SERVICES TO THE VENTURE

When an investor performs services for the venture, and the venture capitalizes their cost, the investor may not recognize profit if the investor controls the venture. If the investor does not control the venture, profit recognition to the extent of outside interests in the venture may be appropriate if all of the following conditions are present:

- The substance of the transaction does not significantly differ from the form;
- The transaction is determined as being on an arm's-length basis. The value of such services must be comparable to the value of similar services to independent third parties;
- There are no substantial uncertainties about the ability of the investor to perform (such as when the investor lacks experience in the business of the venture) or about the total costs of the services he will render;
- The investor performing the services has no other continuing involvement with the venture; and
- The other investors can reasonably be expected to bear their share of venture losses.

The portion of profit to be recognized should be based on performance (costs incurred) or, if the services are similar to a general contractor's, the percentage of completion or completed contract method, as set forth in the AICPA *Industry Audit Guide: Audits of Construction Contractors.* The portion of the profit applicable to the investor's equity should be deferred until the venture charges those costs to operations. An example illustrating sales of services to a venture is set forth in Table 14.3.

VENTURE SELLS REAL ESTATE OR
SERVICES TO INVESTOR

Since an investor cannot recognize profit on a sale of property to itself, the investor must defer its interest (proportionate share) in the venture

Table 14.3. Sales of Services to the Venture

Assumptions

1. Investors *A, B, C,* and *D* form a venture in which each has a 25% interest to construct and sell condominiums. Investor *A*, an experienced general contractor, serves as the general contractor for the project and is compensated on a basis comparable to arrangements with independent third parties, that is, at 5% of construction costs.
2. Investor *A*'s fee and profit is determined as follows:

Total construction costs	$2,500,000
Compensation rate	5%
Total fee to be paid Investor *A*	$ 125,000
Less costs incurred	75,000
Investor A's profit on such services	$ 50,000

3. The venture capitalizes its cost of these services.
4. Investor *A* incurs costs as follows: Year 1—$45,000 (60%); Year 2—$30,000 (40%).
5. The project was sold out in Year 2.

Accounting by the Investor

Investor *A* may recognize profit to the extent of the other investors' interest (75% × $50,000 = $37,500) as the services are rendered. The remaining profit ($50,000 − $37,500 = $12,500) should be recognized in Year 2 when the venture charges such costs to cost of sales. Accordingly, Investor *A*'s profit recognition in each year is calculated as follows:

	Profit Recognized		
Year	As services are rendered	As costs are charged to expense by venture	Total
1	$22,500 (60%)		$22,500
2	15,000 (40%)	$12,500	27,500
	$37,500	$12,500	$50,000

If, under a different arrangement, Investor *A* controls the venture, he would be required to defer recognition of the entire $50,000 profit until Year 2, when sale of the entire project is completed.

profit. The investor's share of this income should be treated as a reduction in the carrying amount of the purchased property and recognized as the asset if depreciated or sold to a third party.

If the venture performs services for the investor and the investor capitalizes the costs, the above general rule for a sale of real estate would be equally applicable. The capitalized costs should be reduced by the investor's interest in the venture's profit on the services performed. An example to illustrate a sale from the venture to investor is set forth in Table 14.4.

Table 14.4. Sale of Real Estate from a Venture to an Investor

---

Assumptions
1. Venture ABC sells undeveloped land, having a cost basis of $200,000, to Investor *A* for $350,000. Investor *A* plans to subdivide the property into lots.
2. Investor *A* has a one-third interest in Venture ABC.

Accounting by the Investor
Investor *A*'s carrying value in the property is determined as follows:

Purchase price	$350,000
Less—Investor *A*'s equity in the profit realized by Venture ABC ($350,000 less $200,000 × 33⅓%)	50,000
Investor *A*'s carrying value	$300,000

Investor *A* would, subsequently, recognize the $50,000 profit deferred upon sale of the individual lots to third parties.

Chapter 15

Special Investor Accounting Problems

There are a number of other investor accounting problems that require special treatment and attention. They include:

Lag in venture reporting;

Accounting for the difference between the carrying amount of an investment in a venture and the underlying equity in net assets;

Sale of an interest in a venture; and

Income tax provision on undistributed venture earnings.

These problems are covered in the following discussion.

LAG IN VENTURE REPORTING

A real estate venture too often has a fiscal year different from that of the investor. In this situation it is, of course, preferable for the financial statements of the venture to be prepared using the same reporting period as that of the investor for the purposes of inclusion in the investor's financial statements. In many situations, however, this may be unreasonable or impractical. In such cases, the fiscal year of the venture is used, but there will be an interim period between the fiscal year-end of the venture and that of the investor. When such a lag exists, intervening events materially affecting the financial position or results of operations of the venture and the investor should be analyzed to determine whether or not the financial statements of the investor should be adjusted or whether disclosures of such events are necessary.

Authoritative literature gives some guidance in this area. Paragraph 19g of *Accounting Principles Board Opinion No. 18* provides guidance relative to the equity method of accounting by stating:

> . . . if financial statements of an investee are not sufficiently timely for an investor to apply the equity method currently, the investor ordinarily should record its share of the earnings or losses of an investee from the most recent available financial statements.

This statement implies that the unavailability of timely information may not, in itself, be given as a reason for not applying the equity method to otherwise qualifying investments. The opinion does not specify what is considered to be an acceptable lag. However, the provision relating to consolidation of subsidiaries with fiscal years different from the parent company that is set out in *Accounting Research Bulletin* (ARB) *No. 51,* paragraph 4 provides a reasonable guideline by indicating that the difference in fiscal periods should normally not exceed three months. Of course, in applying these guidelines judgment must be exercised and the financial statements of the investor must be fairly presented in accordance with generally accepted accounting principles.

ACCOUNTING FOR THE DIFFERENCE BETWEEN THE CARRYING AMOUNT OF AN INVESTMENT IN A. VENTURE AND THE UNDERLYING EQUITY IN NET ASSETS

Differences between an investor's carrying value of an investment in a real estate venture as compared to its equity in the underlying net assets of the venture may exist for a number of reasons. For example, differences may result from differing accounting methods used by the investor and the venture, or the investor may have unrecognized profits on transfers of real estate to the venture.

Differences could also exist upon acquisition of a venture interest subsequent to the formation of the venture. In this case, the excess cost of the acquired investment over the equity in the underlying assets usually is attributable to the fair values of property interest owned by the venture. If the excess cannot be attributed to such real estate assets, because of the limited life and limited purpose usually inherent in real estate ventures, the excess should be amortized. This is done either in relation to the depreciation of the real estate assets or in relation to the cost of sales depending on the nature of the venture's business.

AICPA *Statement of Position 78–9* indicates that the period of amortization in such circumstances should not exceed 40 years. All such differences should be appropriately recognized on the equity basis as an adjustment to the investor's share of the income or loss of the venture. An example illustrating this principle is set forth in Table 15.1.

Table 15.1. Differences Between Carrying Value and Equity

Assumptions
1. Investor *A* acquired a one-third interest in Venture XYZ for $500,000 cash. Venture XYZ's principal purpose is to operate an office building. At the time of purchase, recorded net assets of the venture totaled $1,200,000 (compared to a fair value of $1,500,000), indicating that the acquired interest had a net book value of $400,000 (⅓ of $1,200,000). Further, assume that the fair value of the land portion is the same as the book value.
2. Investor *A*'s balance sheet before and after recording the foregoing transaction is illustrated in part below:

	Before	After
Cash	$500,000	–
Investment in Venture XYZ	–	$500,000

Accounting by the Investor
The excess purchase price of $100,000 over Investor *A*'s $400,000 share of the net book value is to be amortized. The excess is, in substance, an adjustment to the venture's cost basis in the real estate owned as it constitutes the venture's only asset. Consequently, for the purposes of Investor *A*'s accounting for its investment in Venture XYZ, the $100,000 would be amortized in the same manner as depreciation of the improvements over the remaining useful life of the office building until the building is sold or otherwise disposed of by the venture or Investor *A* sells his interest in the venture.

SALE OF AN INTEREST IN A VENTURE

A sale of an investment in a real estate venture is in substance a sale of an investment in the underlying real estate. It should be evaluated in the context of the guidelines set forth in accounting for sales of real estate. Subject to those guidelines, gain or loss on the sale of the investment should be recognized. The gain or loss is the difference between the selling price and the investor's carrying amount at the time of sale. Of course, book/tax timing differences and the related deferred taxes that have been accrued should be taken into account.

INCOME TAX PROVISION ON
UNDISTRIBUTED VENTURE EARNINGS

Unincorporated Ventures. Such as general partnerships, limited partnerships, and undivided interests, are not directly subject to income taxes. Taxable income or loss from the venture's operations is recognized in the income tax returns of the investors. Therefore, with regard to investor accounting for income taxes directly related to its interest, the investor must provide for taxes on its equity in venture profits as reported in the investor's financial statements. Appropriate income tax allocation principles should be utilized to account for book/tax timing differences.

Corporate Ventures. Are subject to income taxes and, therefore, require different guidelines. If the investor currently recognizes its share of the earnings of a corporate venture and such earnings are not distributed currently by the venture, a book/tax timing difference occurs. This is because income reported currently in the investor's financial statements is taxable income when it is received as a dividend or realized by a sale of the investor's interest in the venture. The question arises as to whether taxes that would be payable if such earnings are realized in a taxable transaction should be recorded in the same period that earnings are reported.

Accounting Principles Board Opinion No. 23, "Accounting for Income Taxes—Special Areas," provides guidelines by stating that generally deferred taxes should be provided on undistributed venture earnings at the time the earnings are included in the investor's income if both of the following conditions are present:

- The corporate venture has a life limited by the nature of the venture, project or other business activity; and

- It can, therefore, reasonably be presumed that the earnings of such a venture will be transferred to the investor in a taxable distribution.

If the corporate venture is essentially permanent in duration, then an analysis must be made to determine the portion which:

- Evidence shows has been or will be invested indefinitely in the venture or which will be remitted in a tax-free liquidation; or
- Is expected to be transferred to the investor in a taxable transaction. Deferred taxes should be provided on this portion.

The investor should determine the amount of deferred taxes by computing the additional income taxes that would have been payable. The additional taxes are computed at normal rates allowing for foreign tax credits or dividends received, deductions where applicable, or capital gains rates, whichever is appropriate. It is assumed that the earnings were distributed as a dividend or the investments were sold in the current period, and, also, that the investor used all available tax-planning alternatives and available tax credits and deductions.

PART FOUR

FINANCIAL REPORTING AND ANALYSIS

Chapter 16

Financial Reporting

Information essential for a fair presentation of the financial statement must be provided. This information is, basically, that which is required by generally accepted accounting principles and that which might affect the conclusions drawn by a reasonably informed reader. The information should be presented in such a manner that its significance is apparent. The financial reporting guidelines in this chapter are based on the principles set forth in authoritative literature and the reporting practices determined from recent annual surveys conducted by the author.

FINANCIAL STATEMENT PRESENTATION

There are a number of matters on financial statement presentation—as opposed to footnote disclosures—that are unique to the real estate industry. The areas set forth following relate to presentations in the balance sheet, income statement, and the statement of changes in financial position.

Presentation of Current Assets and Liabilities

Typically, the balance sheets of real estate companies do not distinguish between current and noncurrent assets and liabilities. *Accounting Research Bulletin No. 43,* Chapter 3A, "Current Assets and Current Liabilities," emphasizes that in determining current assets and liabilities, the criteria developed must relate to the operating cycle of the business. The operating cycle is defined as the average time intervening between the acquisition of materials or services entering the business process and the final cash realization. The *Bulletin* further states:

A one-year time period is to be used as a basis for the segregation of current assets in cases where there are several operating cycles occurring within a year. However, where the period of the operating cycle is more than twelve months, as in, for instance, the tobacco, distillery, and lumber businesses, the longer period should be used. Where a particular business has no clearly defined operating cycle, the one-year rule should govern.

While the operating cycle of a real estate entity ordinarily exceeds one year, it is not possible, in most instances, to clearly define the cycle. Therefore, the classification of current assets and liabilities on the basis of the one-year rule would not be meaningful for most real estate companies. Both the *Accounting Research Bulletin* and the SEC Regulation S-X recognize that there may be exceptions to the general rule. SEC Regulation S-X provides some guidelines for disclosure when a company elects to present a classified balance sheet based on an operating cycle that exceeds more than one year.

Recent surveys of accounting and reporting practices of real estate developers showed that less than 20 percent used a balance sheet that distinguished between current and noncurrent assets and liabilities. All others used an unclassified balance sheet.

Arrangement of Assets

The predominant method for real estate companies is to arrange assets in the order of liquidity. (That means the order of expected conversion to cash.) A second method is to arrange the assets in the order of significance to the company's operations. Thus, the first assets listed might be "real estate" or "properties."

Presentation of Real Estate Assets

Real estate assets should be grouped and presented to assist the reader of the financial statements to better understand the operations and financial position of the business. Real estate assets are usually grouped according to general classifications:

Unimproved land;
Land under development;

Residential lots;

Condominium;

Single-family dwellings; or

Rental properties.

Significant write-downs should be reflected in the income statement as a single-line item.

Offsetting Nonrecourse Debt Against Real Estate Properties

In the real estate industry, debt agreements secured by real property often give the lender no recourse against the debtor in the event of default. When a default occurs, the lender can only seek to take possession of and title to the related real property in settlement of the debt. Although some accountants believe that the property should be presented net of the non-recourse debt in the financial statements, neither the accounting literature, as described following, nor current practice supports such offsetting.

Some developers, however, do disclose in a note to the financial statements the amount of, and the interrelationship of, the nonrecourse debt with the cost of the related properties.

Authoritative Literature. The AICPA *Accounting Guide: Accounting for Retail Land Sales* states:

> If long-term debt or other liabilities may be satisfied by relinquishing title to property without exposure to deficiency judgment, the amounts of those liabilities and the assets subject to the liens should be appropriately disclosed. Netting or offsetting of the liabilities against the related assets is not appropriate.

Further, Topic 10E of the SEC's *Staff Accounting Bulletin No. 1* also indicates that offsetting is not appropriate:

> Carrying values of properties should not be reduced by purchase money mortgages even if the liability on such a mortgage is only a liability against the property. When a registrant sells property subject to a mort-gage and takes from the purchaser a wrap-around mortgage which pro-

vides that the registrant's balance sheet should show the wrap-around mortgage as a receivable. The balance of the previously existing mortgage should not be offset against the receivable on the wrap-around mortgage.

Sources of Income

As a general rule, it is appropriate to classify revenue and cost of sales or operations by principal sources or type of activity. Typically, these classifications will be similar to those used for the aforementioned real estate assets. This disclosure helps the reader to better understand the results of operations of the business.

Financial Reporting of Business Segments

In December 1976, the FASB issued *Statement of Financial Accounting Standards No. 14*, "Financial Reporting for Segments of a Business Enterprise," which requires, among other things, that financial statements disclose certain information relating to an enterprise's operations in different industries, its foreign operations and export sales, and its major customers. For each separate reportable industry segment, as defined therein, the following information has to be disclosed and reconciled to related amounts in the financial statements of the enterprise as a whole:

- Revenue—sales to unaffiliated customers and intersegment sales or transfers;
- Profitability—operating profit or loss and comments on any unusual or infrequently occurring items;
- Identifiable assets; and
- Other related disclosures, including aggregate amount of depreciation, depletion, and amortization expense, capital expenditures, and effects of accounting changes.

The Statement also requires that an enterprise operating predominantly or exclusively in a single industry identify that industry in lieu of presenting the previous information for separate reportable industry segments.

Recent survey results are summarized here:

	Number of companies
Real estate business segments specifically identified:	
• Two or more real estate segments	17
• Single real estate segment predominant	15
• Diversified company with single real estate segment	9
Predominant real estate segment implicit from annual report disclosures	19
Business segment disclosure requirements not required—year-end prior to effective date	30
Total	90

Cash Flow Versus Earnings Per Share

SEC *Accounting Series Release No. 142* indicates that per share data, other than that relating to net income, net assets and dividends, should be avoided in reporting financial results. The ASR was issued to limit certain presentations of per share data relating to cash flow.

Real Estate Ventures

As discussed on page 155, a controlling investor usually is required to consolidate venture operations. An exception to this general rule is also discussed on page 155. When consolidation is not required, the cost or equity method should be applied as appropriate under the circumstances.

Equity Method. Under the equity method, the financial statements should use the one-line approach, with the carrying value of the investment presented as a single amount in the investor's balance sheet, and the investor's share of venture earnings or losses as a single amount in the income statement. An illustration of the equity method is presented in Table 16.1.

A noncontrolling investor should use the equity method (one-line approach), as described previously, except where the cost method is appropriate or where the proportionate share method may be appropriate in the rare situation where the stringent criteria for "undivided interest" are met.

Paragraph 19c of *APB No. 18* (which, by the November 1971 Accounting Interpretation, may be considered applicable to partnerships and unincorporated joint ventures) states:

Table 16.1   One-Line Approach—Equity Method

Assumptions
  (1) *A* invests $200,000 to purchase a 25% interest in a corporate venture.
  (2) *A* is a real estate owner and operator.
  (3) The venture was formed to acquire and operate an income producing property.
  (4) For the purpose of the example, earnings are assumed to be distributed in the future on a tax-free basis. (See page 178, "Income Tax Provision on Undistributed Venture Earnings.")

	Investor *A*	Corporate venture
Rental income	$2,000,000	$800,000
Operating expenses and depreciation	1,600,000	700,000
	400,000	100,000
Income taxes (say 55%)	220,000	55,000
Net income	$ 180,000	$ 45,000

Reporting by the Investor
  Investor *A* would report combined operations as follows:

Income statement	
Rental income	$2,000,000
Operating expenses and depreciation	1,600,000
	400,000
Income taxes	220,000
Income before equity in earnings of 25% owned venture	180,000
Equity in earnings of venture (25% of $45,000)	11,250
Net income	$ 191,250
Balance sheet	
Investment in venture ($200,000 plus $11,250)	$ 211,250

The investment(s) in common stock should be shown in the balance sheet of an investor as a single amount, and the investor's share of earnings or losses of an investee(s) should ordinarily be shown in the income statement as a single amount except for . . . extraordinary items.

Statement of Position 78–9 further emphasizes that the one-line approach must be used for all entities except where the above exceptions exist.

It should be noted that paragraph 19d of the *Accounting Principles Board Opinion No. 18* requires the investor's share of extraordinary items and its share of prior period adjustments that are reported in the venture's financial statements to be classified in a similar manner by the investor unless they are immaterial in the investor's income statement.

If the joint venture were a partnership, the investor's share of the venture income may be included in operating income before income taxes, since the venture income is included in determining the income tax provision of the investor.

Proportionate Share Approach—Undivided Interests. According to the November 1971 interpretation to *APB No. 18,* this method may be applied first, to noncorporate investments which are, in fact, undivided interests (each participant owns an undivided interest in each venture asset and is liable for a proportionate share of each liability), and secondly, where it has become established industry practice. This may be the case for oil and gas and mining ventures or for similar ventures that are a part of a vertically integrated operation. Generally, this feature of being part of a vertically integrated operation, which makes the proportionate share approach appropriate, is not found in real estate operations.

The proportionate share approach is to record the investor's share of each item of income, expense, asset and liability, together with appropriate interentity eliminations.

This approach in a venture's balance sheet should be applied selectively even for legally undivided interests because the concept of proportionate title may not be valid. A partner may not be able to exercise his title to a portion of each asset because of an agreement or practical business considerations and there is no product which is shared by the investor.

Another problem in using this method is that the interests of the other investors are not disclosed and the statements may imply, erroneously, that all assets are under unrestricted control of the investor. On the other hand, where the investors have guaranteed the debt of the venture, the share of the debt might well be recorded by the investor and his investment increased accordingly.

Combination Approach. The combination approach uses the one-line method for the balance sheet and the proportionate share method for the income statement. Although this approach has, previously, found acceptance in practice in the real estate industry, at least with respect to unincorporated ventures, *Statement of Position 78–9* clearly indicates that the combination approach is not acceptable in the real estate industry.

Statement of Changes in Financial Position

APB 19, "Reporting Changes in Financial Position," requires that a statement summarizing the changes in financial position be presented as a basic financial statement for each period for which an income statement is presented. Statements of changes in financial position of real estate companies usually comprise changes in cash rather than changes in working capital. Real estate companies usually do not distinguish between current and noncurrent assets and liabilities.

Regarding estate ventures, *Statement of Position 78–9* narrows the alternatives that were formerly used in presenting an investor's share of a real estate venture's earnings under the equity method in the investor's statement of changes in financial position. It stipulates that, in arriving at working capital or cash provided by operations, only earnings distributed (or accrued as a receivable in accordance with generally accepted accounting principles) during the period may be included in the determinations.

This restriction does not preclude, however, the practice of deducting equity in earnings from venture operations when determining working capital or cash provided by operations and presenting dividends received as a separate source of funds that are not provided from operations.

Retail Land Developers

Financial statement presentation for companies that are required to comply with the *Retail Land Sales Guide* are set forth in detail in the exhibits to that guide. Financial statement presentation for this unique segment of the real estate industry, therefore, is not described in this book.

ACCOUNTING POLICIES

Because of the many alternatives currently available in accounting for real estate developments, it is especially important to follow the guidelines of *Accounting Principles Board Opinion No. 22*, "Disclosure of Accounting Policies." It states, in part, that disclosures should encompass those accounting principles and method that involve any of the following:

- A selection from existing acceptable alternatives;
- Principles and methods peculiar to the industry in which the reporting entity operates, even if such principles and methods are predominantly followed in that industry; or
- Unusual or innovative applications of generally accepted accounting principles and, as applicable, of principles and methods peculiar to the industry in which the reporting entity operates.

The following is a discussion of certain accounting policy disclosures that are appropriate in the financial statements of a real estate developer, as opposed to a manufacturing or service enterprise.

Principles of Profit Recognition

The following disclosures on principles of profit recognition should be included:

- The method of income recognition (for example, completed contract, percentage of completion, installment method, cost recovery method):
  - When more than one method is utilized, disclosure should be made of the circumstance under which each method is used;
  - When the percentage of completion method is used, disclosure should be made of the basis (for example, cost incurred, engineering estimates). In the case of condominiums, disclosure is typically made of the minimum requirements for both units sold and construction costs incurred in a project before profit is recognized;
- The time of recording the sale and the related profit (for example, at the time of closing or at the time title passes); and

- The interest rates used when the initial valuation of the consideration includes imputation of interest.

Cost Accounting Policies

Financial statement disclosure should include, where applicable and significant, capitalization policies for property taxes and other carrying costs, and policies on capitalization or deferral of start-up or preoperating costs—for example, selling costs, rental costs, and initial operations. The method of allocating cost to unit sales should also be disclosed—for example, relative market value, area, unit, and specific identification.

Market or Net Realizable Value

The method of determining market or net realizable value preferably should be disclosed since inventory is required to be carried at the lower of cost or net realizable value.

Investments in Real Estate Ventures

The following disclosures of accounting policies should be made:

- The method of inclusion in investor's accounts—for example, one line, consolidation;
- The method of income recognition—for example, equity, cost;
- Accounting principles of significant ventures;
- Profit recognition principles on transactions between the investor and the venture.

OTHER DISCLOSURES

The following discussion describes some other financial statement disclosures, usually in footnotes, which are appropriate in the financial statements of a real estate developer.

Real Estate Assets

If a breakdown is not reflected on the balance sheet, as previously described, it should be included in the footnotes. Disclosure should also be made of the inventory subject to sales contracts that has not been recorded as sales and the portion of inventory serving as collateral for debts.

Summarized information or explanations about significant inventory write-downs should be disclosed in the footnotes as write-downs that are generally important and unusual items.

Although it is not considered appropriate to offset nonrecourse debt against the related asset, it would be appropriate to disclose in a note to the financial statements the amount and interrelationship of the nonrecourse debt with the cost of the related property.

Capitalization of Interest

Financial Accounting Standards No. 34, "Capitalization of Interest Cost," requires the disclosure of the amount of interest expensed and the amount capitalized.

Deferral of Sales Recognition

Financial statements should include disclosure of the accounting method that is followed when major sale transactions do not qualify as sales for financial reporting purposes. In circumstances where the deposit method is appropriate, such disclosures usually should indicate that, until a transaction qualifies as a sale, all payments received are recorded as deposits. Also, if the property "sold" and any related mortgage debt are not segregated and separately identified on the balance sheet as being subject to sales contracts, the information should be disclosed in the footnotes. Notes receivable arising from the transaction should not be reflected on the balance sheet.

If sales transactions that are not recorded are material, notes to the financial statements should also disclose:

(1) the nature of the transaction;
(2) the method of accounting being used;
(3) the amounts of contracts not recorded as sales and unrecorded mortgage notes receivable; and
(4) any other information deemed necessary for complete disclosure.

Deferral of Profit Recognition

When transactions qualify as sales for accounting purposes (but do not meet the tests for full profit recognition) and the installment or cost recovery method of accounting is used, disclosure should be made of significant amounts of profit deferred, the nature of the transaction and any other information deemed necessary for complete disclosure.

Sales to Related Parties

AICPA *Statement of Auditing Standards No. 6,* "Related Party Transaction," provides guidance on disclosures that should be considered in connection with related party sales transactions. It is particularly pertinent because real estate developers frequently are involved with related parties. Related parties, generally, include affiliates, principal owners, directors, trustees, officers, members of their immediate families, and other parties where either party has the ability to significantly influence the other. Related party transactions would also include sales to entities in which the seller has an equity interest. The statement indicates:

> Disclosure in financial statements of a reporting entity that has participated in related party transactions that are material, individually or in the aggregate, should include the following:
> (a) The nature of the relationship(s).
> (b) A description of the transactions (summarized when appropriate) for the period reported on, including amounts, if any, and such other information as is deemed necessary to an understanding of the effects on the financial statements.
> (c) The dollar volume of transactions and the effects of any change in the method of establishing terms from that used in the preceding period.
> (d) Amounts due from or to related parties and, if not otherwise apparent, the terms and manner of settlement.

Disclosure of significant income recognized on sales to related parties is particularly important.

Real Estate Ventures

Typical disclosures regarding real estate ventures are:

- Names of significant ventures, percentage of ownership interest, cash distribution arrangements, and profit participations for accounting and tax purposes;
- Nature of operations and significant provisions of venture agreements;

- Accounting and tax policies, including the principles of profit recognition on transactions between the investor and the venture and income recognized if a major transaction is involved;
- Differences, if any, between the carrying amount of the investment in the financial statements and the investor's share of equity in net assets and the accounting policy regarding amortization of the difference;
- Summarized information about assets, liabilities, and results of operations or separate financial statements of ventures and the investor's interest; and
- Investor commitments with respect to joint ventures.

Most of these disclosures are required by paragraph 20 of *Accounting Principles Board Opinion No. 18* for investments which are significant, either individually or in the aggregate, to an investor's financial statements.

Commitments and Contingencies

Exceptionally large commitments, particularly those arising other than in the ordinary course of business, should be disclosed. These commitments might include those to purchase (or construct) real estate, to purchase long-term investments, or to provide financing to affiliates—including joint ventures—and to guarantee debt of others.

Real estate companies often sell properties subject to permanent mortgages. When a company remains contingently liable for such mortgages assumed by others, the amounts of the mortgages should be disclosed, if material.

Uncertainties

In 1974 the SEC issued *Accounting Series Release No. 166,* "Disclosure of Unusual Risks and Uncertainties in Financial Reporting," which states:

> . . . when unusual circumstances arise or where there are significant changes in the degree of business uncertainty existing in a reporting entity, a registrant has the responsibility of communicating these items in its financial statements. It is not sufficient to assume that the numbers shown in conventional fashion on the face of the financial statements will adequately inform investors. The basic accounting model is by its very nature a single valued one in which a single best estimate is reflected in

the face of the statements. While in most cases this presentation effectively communicates business financial position and results of operations, under some conditions of major uncertainty it may not adequately inform investors of the realities of a business being reported. In such cases, registrants must consider the need for substantial and specific disclosure of such uncertainties and, in extreme cases, the need for deviation from the conventional reporting model. In addition, independent public accountants must consider the need for disclosure of such uncertainties in their report.

The SEC release contains a list of specific examples not intended to be all inclusive. One of the examples given, however, appears to apply directly to certain developers, such as a developer with one or a small number of projects that will have a dominant effect in determining the company's success or failure. The release states that, in such cases, estimates of future success may be necessary in order to present financial statements on a going concern basis. In addition, the degree of that future success may have to be predicted, to some explicit degree, in order to present an income statement covering current operations. Accounting for developments requires a number of estimates such as a sales price, the sales pace, and the effect of changing levels of costs—including inflation. The release states that in situations in which one or a few estimates subject to substantial uncertainty will have a dominant effect, disclosure of the sensitivity of the results to estimates must be emphasized. In addition, under unusual circumstances, substantial footnote discussion of results under alternative assumptions should be considered.

While this SEC release is applicable only to SEC reporting companies, the disclosure guidelines should be considered applicable to all companies.

Troubled Debt Restructuring

The nature of a real estate developer's operations is such that assets are generally leveraged with large amounts of debt and, depending on the success of a particular development, are prone to restructuring arrangements. *Financial Accounting Statement No. 15,* "Accounting by Debtors and Creditors for Troubled Debt Restructurings," requires the following disclosures by the debtor about troubled debt restructurings that occur during the periods for which the financial statements are presented.

- A description of the principal changes in terms for each restructuring, the major features of settlement, or both;

- Aggregate gain on restructuring of payables and the related income tax effect;

- Aggregate net gain or loss on transfers of assets recognized during the period; and

- Per share amount of the aggregate gain on restructuring of payables, net of related income tax effect.

A debtor must disclose the extent to which amounts contingently payable are included in the carrying amount of restructured payables. A debtor must also disclose unrecorded amounts that are contingently payable on restructured payables. In both situations, conditions under which those amounts would become payable or would be forgiven should be disclosed.

Retail Land Developers

Financial statement disclosures for companies which must comply with the *Retail Land Guide* are set forth in detail in the exhibits to the AICPA industry accounting guide. Therefore, disclosures for this unique segment of the real estate industry are not discussed here.

Construction Contractors

The principal reporting considerations for construction contractors relate to the two methods of income recognition: the percentage of completion method and the completed contract method.

When the completed contract method is used, an excess of accumulated costs over related billings should be shown in a classified balance sheet as a current asset, and an excess of accumulated billings over related costs should be shown as a current liability. If costs exceed billings on some contracts, and billings exceed costs on others, the contracts should ordinarily be segregated so that the asset side includes only those contracts on which costs exceed billings, and the liability side includes only those on which billings exceed costs.

Under the percentage of completion method, assets may include costs and related income not yet billed with respect to certain contracts. Liabilities may include billings in excess of costs and related income with respect to other contracts.

Chapter 17

Financial Analysis

Traditionally, real estate investors have been concerned primarily with cash flow, appreciation potential, and tax shelter opportunities. The statement of income and the balance sheet prepared on the basis of generally accepted accounting principles, however, do not meet these needs and are not very useful in assessing these attributes of a real estate investment. It has been asserted that generally accepted accounting principles distort results of operations of real estate and, thus, assessment of performance requires special analysis. Some public real estate companies have been so disenchanted with accounting practices required under generally accepted accounting principles that they have gone so far as to "go private" or leave the real estate business.

Investors in income properties are much more interested in cash flow. Depreciation is not a cash outlay. On the other hand, amortization payments on the mortgage debt are cash outlays. Since the traditional accounting model usually has a higher amount of depreciation in the early years, as compared to principal amortization, net income would normally be significantly less than cash flow—and perhaps misleading.

In addition to these fundamental problems, different accounting policies exist among real estate companies. These differences include items such as start-up and preoperating costs, selling costs, and interest costs prior to the effects of FAS 34. Some companies expense these costs while others capitalize them, based on differing criteria. Further, depreciation lives and methods vary considerably. It is no surprise then, that comparisons between companies, even on an historical cost basis, have been difficult.

Some investors put money in real estate tax shelters, as described on page 3 in Chapter 1. Although the investors are interested in cash flow and appreciation, their more immediate interests are usually in tax losses that can be used to offset income from other sources.

CASH FLOW

Basic financial statements under generally accepted accounting principles require a statement summarizing changes in financial position for each period for which an income statement is presented. To meet this requirement, many real estate entities show changes in cash. The frequent reason for this is that they believe that cash flow presentation is more appropriate; but it should also be pointed out that many real estate entities do not present assets and liabilities classified as current or noncurrent. Generally, however, they believe that the statement of cash flow does not get sufficient attention from the reader of the financial statement.

Because many real estate entities have been unhappy with depreciation and other noncash charges to income, they have included various kinds of cash flow information elsewhere in their annual reports. They have used terminology such as "earnings before noncash charges," "cash flow," and "net operating income." Some included cash flow per share data. The AICPA Accounting Principles Board in 1971 issued *Opinion No. 19,* "Reporting Changes in Financial Position," which strongly recommended in paragraph 15 that cash flow per share should not be presented in annual reports to shareholders. The use of "cash flow per share" data also led the SEC to issue in 1973 *Accounting Series Release No. 142,* "Reporting Cash Flow and Other Related Data." It prohibited the reporting of per share data other than that relating to net income, net assets, and/or dividends. It also imposed other restrictions, stating:

> Until new and uniform measurement principles are developed and approved for an industry, the presentation of measures of performance other than net income should be approached with extreme caution. Such measures should not be presented in a manner which gives them greater authority or prominence than conventionally computed earnings.

Experimentation with cash flow information reporting was somewhat curtailed, but many companies found innovative ways of disclosing the information in their annual reports. For example, a number of companies presented the information in financial highlights and results of operations. Still others gave the information in the president's or chairman's letter to shareholders.

DEPRECIATION

There are many reasons why traditional cost basis financial statements fall short of investors' needs. One which is often cited relates to depreciation of income properties. While accountants record depreciation (as required under generally accepted accounting principles), investors contend that with real estate there frequently is appreciation in value. They are often correct in their contentions.

What's wrong with depreciation? Customarily, there is a single one-time major investment for an income property. Large portions of it are nonrenewable and maintenance-free. In an apartment project, improvements such as the carpets, stoves, heating system, plumbing, air conditioner, roof and even the sidewalks can be renewed, repaired, or replaced. The building's shell, however, is not renewable. The shell would include the structure, brickwork, ducts, and foundation. The shell does not deteriorate and it is not replaced. It is virtually maintenance-free. Both the building shell and the land are subject to economic depreciation (or appreciation), but not to physical depreciation.

Traditional accounting does not take into consideration the physical characteristic of a building's shell. Nor does it recognize the significance of a single one-time major investment that will provide relatively stable income for a long period of time. The real estate investor knows the shell can stand forever in physical terms. When an alternative use for the land promises a greater cash return, the building may be replaced—but frequently at a gain to the investor.

The investor knows that he must continually maintain and modernize the property or he will lose revenue. When a property does decline in value because it can't produce enough income, the investor often assumes that increasing land values will cover any loss. If the property's value consists of ten percent land and ninety percent improvements, the value of the land could easily increase at an average rate of six percent a year. In 40 years, the investor would fully recover the original value of the buildings from the land appreciation alone.

Some accountants have proposed the sinking fund method of depreciation that results in increasing depreciation charges with the passage of time. The rationale for the sinking fund method is based principally on the fact that in many situations it normalizes the aggregate of depreciation and interest expense, producing an income charge almost identical to cash payments for debt service. The sinking fund method may be theoretically justifiable, but in the light of actual practice, it is artificial and contrived. Real estate investors do not use a depreciation concept in determining the soundness of a potential or existing real estate investment. Their calculations are oriented to cash return.

CURRENT VALUES

The traditional accounting model does not permit recording appreciation of real estate. This problem is most dramatic with respect to depreciable income properties, but it is also important with respect to land. That's because the real estate industry is characterized by a long business cycle. Appreciation is not realized until a sale occurs, usually long after one year. Prior to the time of sale, however, many companies contend economic gains have occurred that should be communicated to readers of financial statements. They have contended that current values of real estate is information of major importance to investors and lenders in judging the present financial position of an entity.

During recent years, numerous real estate companies recorded valuation losses in connection with real estate investments held for sale. Many felt this was oppressively one-sided since they could not use the appreciation of good investments to offset losses that had to be recorded on unsuccessful projects. Nonetheless, they have had to live with the historical cost basis financial statements.

Reporting of Current Value Information

In 1976 the SEC issued *Accounting Series Release 190,* revoked in 1979, which included requirements for disclosure of the replacement cost of productive assets. This led to renewed interest in the presentation of current value information in the financial statements of public companies. Previously, a few real estate companies had reported certain current value information, but only outside of the financial statements.

The SEC gave several real estate companies permission to disclose current value financial information and encouraged experimentation in this area. As a result, some began to include a current value basis balance sheet in their annual report to shareholders, with the information presented in comparative form along with the historical cost basis balance sheet. A few other companies chose the footnote disclosure of current values.

The current value balance sheets reflected amounts in considerable excess of historical cost. The excess has been described by terms such as "revaluation equity" or "unrealized appreciation." The current value balance sheet has usually been accompanied by a statement of changes in revaluation equity from the prior year and a very detailed footnote disclosure of the basis of valuation. Generally, the effect of depreciation or cost of sales on a current value basis in the income statement has not been disclosed.

The appraisal of real estate is inherently highly subjective. In an effort to instill confidence in readers of current value financial statements, the prevalent practice has been for reporting companies to estimate the current values and then have them reviewed by independent real estate appraisers. The reports on current values of both appraisers and independent accountants have been included in the annual reports. An example illustrating a statement of current values is set forth in Table 17.1.

The theoretical problems faced in preparing current value data for real estate are too numerous to cover here, but a few questions are sufficiently important:

- Should costs of disposal, such as sales commissions, be deducted since they would be incurred on realization of current values?
- How should income taxes be determined? Should future taxes be reflected at present value of future estimated payments?
- Should undeveloped land be valued as it presently exists or at the present value of cash flow from planned future development?
- Should the "value" of land under development be determined using the value of raw land plus cost of development?
- Should value of completed income properties be ascertained by separately determining the value of land and projected future cash flow from the building?

The issuance of current value financial statements has been the subject of several articles in business publications. The articles have generally praised the current value balance sheet as providing better information to investors and creditors. In addition, the AICPA issued, in 1978, an exposure draft of a proposed Statement of Position, "Presentation and Disclosure of Supplementary Current Value Information," which deals with the subject in some depth. The author agrees that current value information can be useful information if used with a full understanding of the inherent weaknesses in developing the data.

Proposed AICPA Statement of Position

On January 27, 1978, the AICPA issued for public comment an exposure draft of a proposed Statement of Position, "Presentation and Disclosure of Supplementary Current Value Information." It provides guidance for entities that choose to issue supplementary current value financial statements, either in conjunction with or apart from the conventional financial statements, or that choose to issue piecemeal supplementary current value information in conjunction with the conventional financial statements. The following are the major provisions of the proposed statement:

- Any supplementary current value information should, normally, be presented in comparative form with the prior year's financial information—if it is presented in the conventional financial statements. An exception is permitted if developing prior year amounts is impractical when first reporting current value information;
- A financial statement format of presentation should be used only when the current value information is based on a comprehensive current value measurement approach. Such format should present financial position, results of operations and value changes;
- When current value measurements are used only for selected items, a financial statement format should not be used. A piecemeal presentation of supplementary current value information is acceptable if sufficient descriptions and disclosures are made to prevent such information from being misleading. Current values are required for (a) other directly related information, for example, current value depreciation related to property, plant and equipment current values, and (b) all parts of a financial statement caption, for example, all categories of inventory; and
- Current value information should reflect potential tax effects. Presentations of such information should disclose the amounts of the adjust-

Table 17.1. Sample Statement of Current Values

Office Building Inc.
Balance Sheet
(In thousands)

Assets	Current Value Basis	Historical Cost Basis
Cash	$ 100	$ 100
Office building	9800	5700
Less: accumulated depreciation		(200)
	$9900	$5600
Liabilities and Stockholders' Equity		
Mortgage payable	$4900	$5000
Real estate commissions payable on realization of estimated current values	400	
Income taxes on realization of estimated current values	1120	
Stockholders' equity:		
Common stock	100	100
Retained earnings	500	500
Unrealized appreciation	2880	
	$9900	$5600

Current Value Calculation

1. The estimate of current value for the office building was calculated as follows:

Gross income potential	$2400
Less: 5% vacancy and credit loss	(120)
Estimated gross income	$2280
Less: project operating expenses (excluding interest and depreciation)	1300
Operating income	980
Capitalization rate—10%	÷.10
Estimated current value	$9800

2. The mortgage payable has an interest rate below that currently prevailing in the market and accordingly the debt has been reduced to current value.

3. Management's estimate of unrealized appreciation is summarized as follows:

Table 17.1.   (Continued)

Estimated current value of office building	$9800
Less: estimated real estate commissions on realization of current values	(400)
Add: current value reduction in mortgage payable	100
Adjusted current value of office building	9500
Historical cost of office building, net of accumulated depreciation	(5500)
Unrealized appreciation before income taxes	4000
Less: income taxes at 28% capital gains rate	(1120)
Unrealized appreciation	$2880

Note. It may also be appropriate to deduct debt service from operating income and to value the equity position at an appropriate capitalization rate. The mortgage payable would then be added to the value of the equity position to determine the current value of the office building. In this situation a current value reduction in the mortgage payable is not necessary, as it has already been considered in computing the value of the equity position.

ments of current values to reflect tax effects, the method of determining tax effects, and how the tax effects have been reflected in the presentation.

The exposure draft further indicates that disclosures accompanying the current value information should emphasize the experimental nature as well as the subjectivity and imprecision characterizing the information. In addition, it indicates that at least the following information should be an integral part of current value disclosures:

- Current value information is not required for presentation of financial position in conformity with generally accepted accounting principles;
- An identification of the assets and liabilities that are stated at current value;
- A description of the approach used in arriving at current values, including the basic assumptions on which the computations are based, the methods followed, and an identification of the extent, if any, that an outside expert—such as an appraiser—was used in the development of the data; and

- A description of changes in the approaches or methods followed that materially affect the comparability of the information with that of the preceding period.

The exposure draft does not attempt to resolve all the conceptual issues arising in the preparation of current value information and takes no position as to whether entities should issue current value information. There has been no indication of whether a final Statement of Position will ever be issued. Even if it is never published, it has provided useful guidance while the industry is struggling to present more useful financial information to the investor.

FASB Statement No. 33

In December 1978, the Financial Accounting Standards Board issued an exposure draft of a Statement of Financial Accounting Standards, "Financial Reporting and Changing Prices." The proposed statement, a part of the Board's development of a conceptual framework, was in response to the widely recognized need for disclosures about the effects of inflationary costs on business enterprises. Because the exposure draft introduced new measurement concepts, the Board decided that required disclosures should be presented as supplementary information. This enables preparers, auditors, and users of financial statements to gain experience with those concepts under less rigid guidance than would be required if changes had to be made in basic financial statements.

Recognizing that the exposure draft was general and did not address all problems that may be unique to some assets and some industries, industry task groups were formed to identify special measurement and disclosure problems in six industries and to recommend solutions to those problems. One of the six industries was the real estate industry.

The Real Estate Task Group issued an Interim Report in May 1979. It focused, primarily, on the problems of implementation for income properties because the development, ownership, and operation of these properties is the largest segment of the real estate industry. They concluded that:

(1) the most significant impact of changing prices on the real estate industry is the changes in the value (not cost) of resources; and

(2) the most useful financial information for lenders and investors is the value of resources and operating cash flow generated by income properties.

In summary, the Task Group's report indicated that value measurements should be consistent with the expected method and timing of realizing the values reported. The supplemental disclosure should reflect:

- Current exit value for assets which are to be disposed of in orderly liquidation in the short term;
- Expected exit value in due course of business (net realizable value) for assets which are to be disposed of over longer terms; and
- Present value of expected cash flows, where the value of the asset is to be realized through cash flows over the life of the improvements.

The Task Group concluded that in the context of a value-based framework of financial reporting, depreciation of cost (current or historical) is not relevant. The aggregate of operating cash flow, changes in asset value and other changes in net assets during a reporting period is the most useful measurement of income for real estate activities. They further concluded that:

- Operating results and changes in value should be evaluated in terms of constant dollars to provide an analysis of performance adjusted for general inflation;
- Income taxes should be provided on the excess of the value over the tax basis of assets consistent with the expected method and timing of realizing such values and related tax liabilities; and
- Valuation of undeveloped land should not be required, but experimentation should be encouraged to resolve the issues related to land valuation.

The FASB Statement was issued in its final form in September 1979 as *Statement No. 33*. The Statement, which is applicable only to large public entities, requires such entities to report (a) income from continuing operations adjusted for the effects of general inflation and (b) the purchasing power gain or loss on net monetary items. The Statement also requires such entities to report certain financial information on a current cost basis, but the Board has at this time specifically excluded income producing real estate properties from this requirement.

The Board decided that further studies were necessary to determine the applicability of current cost basis information to income-producing real estate properties. The Board's actions have obviously given consideration to the conclusion of the Real Estate Task Group that changes in value of real estate and operating cash flows are of great significance to readers of real estate financial statements. The Board indicated that the arguments of the Task Group convinced them of the need for further consideration of the possible benefits to be derived from the disclosure of net present values of income producing properties.

The FASB is undertaking studies of the applicability of current costs to income properties, with the assistance of the Task Group, and is expected to publish an exposure draft on the subject in 1980. The current actions of the FASB indicate that there is a possibility that an amendment to FAS 33 will be issued in 1980, substituting current value reporting concepts for current cost presentation regarding income producing real estate properties.

FINANCIAL FORECASTS

Many investors and lenders believe that financial forecasts are also very useful and informative. Historically, forecasts have been either discouraged or prohibited in any public reporting. Based on recent developments, however, there likely will be a significant increase in the presentation of financial forecasts. This should make annual reports more meaningful to the reader.

Although offering circulars for real estate partnership interests have in the past included financial forecasts, it previously was the SEC's long-standing policy not to permit forecasts in prospectuses and reports filed with the Commission. In *Release No. 5581,* in April 1975, the SEC proposed changes in that policy to permit companies to include certain statements regarding future operations in some SEC filings. In that release, the SEC also stated that its public hearings had revealed:

> widespread dissatisfaction with the fact that there are no guidelines or standards that the issuer, the financial analyst or the investor can rely on in issuing or interpreting projections.

In November 1978, the SEC published Guides 5 and 62 and *Release No. 5992* which encouraged inclusion (in an appropriate format) of management's projections of future economic performance in some filings with the Commission. The November 1978 SEC pronouncements also included the following in *Release No. 5992:*

- An outside review of management's projections may furnish additional support for reasonableness;
- Traditionally, projections of revenue, net income and earnings per share are generally considered to be of primary importance. However, additional information may be presented so long as misleading inferences are not made through selective projection of only favorable items;
- A projection may be the most probable specific amount or the most reasonable range. However, ranges should not be so wide as to make the disclosures meaningless;
- Several projections based on varying assumptions may be judged by management to be more meaningful than a single number or range and would be permitted;
- Disclosure of the most significant assumptions is encouraged; and
- Management may be responsible for full and prompt disclosure where it has reason to know such projections no longer have a reasonable basis.

In June 1979, the SEC adopted rules to provide a "safe harbor" from liability under the federal securities laws for projections made in good faith, with a reasonable basis in SEC filings and annual reports to shareholders. The rules also provide that the burden of proof is on the plaintiff to establish the absence of a reasonable basis and good faith. The safe harbor rules cover not only projections of certain financial items, but also statements relating to (a) management plans and objectives, and (b) future economic performance included in management's discussion and analysis of the summary of earnings.

The AICPA has also been active. In March 1975, they published MAS *Guideline Series No. 3,* "Guidelines for Systems for the Preparation of Financial Forecasts." In August 1975 the AICPA also issued *Statement of Position 75–4,* "Presentation and Disclosure of Financial Forecasts," which provides general guidelines as to format, disclosure of assumptions and accounting principles. Some of the guidelines of 75–4 are as follows:

- Financial forecasts estimate the most probable financial position, results of operations, or changes in financial position for one or more future periods. Forecasts are distinguished from financial projections that are estimates of financial results based on assumptions which are not necessarily the most likely;
- Financial forecasts must be prepared on a basis consistent with the generally accepted accounting principles expected to be used in the financial statements over the forecast period;
- Significant assumptions underlying the forecast are required:
  - Assumptions as to which there is a reasonable possibility of the occurrence of a variation that may significantly affect the forecasted results;
  - Assumptions about anticipated conditions that are expected to be significantly different from current conditions, which are not otherwise reasonably apparent;
  - Other matters deemed important to the forecast or to the interpretation of the forecast;
- In certain circumstances, updated financial forecasts must be issued to reflect significant changes in assumptions, actual results, or unanticipated events and circumstances.

In 1979, the AICPA had another project underway to set standards for the accountants' review of financial forecasts.

SUMMARY

The traditional historical cost accounting model has not satisfied the needs of the real estate industry. The matters discussed in this chapter are innovative experiments in attempts to solve some of the shortcomings. However, the ultimate solution is elusive, and it should not be expected in the near future. Nonetheless, it is essential that continued improvements be made in order to provide all of the information that investors need for sound investment decisions.

Glossary of Real Estate Words and Phrases

Abstract of title. A summary of the conveyances, transfers, and any other facts relied on as evidence of title, together with any other matters of public record which may impair title.

All-inclusive trust deed. A mortgage subordinate to, but inclusive of, an existing mortgage(s) on a property. In general, a third-party lender refinances the property by extending to the borrower an amount equal to the difference between the face amount on the new mortgage and the balance outstanding on the existing mortgage(s). This difference is, in effect, a junior mortgage. Similar to a *wrap-around mortgage*.

Amenities. Improvements such as utilities, golf courses, clubhouses, swimming pools and tennis courts.

Appraisal. An estimate or opinion of value. The act or process of estimating value.

Appraiser. One who estimates value, specifically one who possesses the necessary qualifications, ability, and experience to execute or direct the appraisal of real or personal property.

Balloon payment. This slang term refers to the unamortized principal amount of a mortgage or term loan which is paid off, in a lump sum, at the end of the term.

Burn-off. Amortization of prepayments such as interest.

Closing. A meeting of the parties to execute and deliver mortgage and/or property title documents.

Common costs. Costs which benefit more than one portion of a project or more than one project within a development. Examples could include hallways and elevators contained in a *condominium,* streets, parking areas and *amenities.* See also *offsite costs.*

Commitment fee.   The fee, frequently a percentage of the expected loan, paid by a borrower to a lender for agreeing to make funds available at a future date.

Completed contract method.   A method of revenue recognition used in connection with long-term construction contracts; normally used when progress toward completion cannot be reasonably estimated. Under this method, revenue and related costs are recognized in the period when the project is completed or substantially completed.

Condominium.   A multiunit structure in which persons hold *fee simple title* to individual units (apartments) together with an undivided interest in the common elements associated with the structure.

Construction loan.   Financing arranged for the construction of real property. It is generally short-term in nature and usually repaid with the proceeds from permanent financing. Construction loans are further defined by whether or not the borrower has a commitment for permanent financing when the construction loan matures. Loans with a permanent financing commitment are designated as "with a take-out commitment" and those which do not have such financing are "without a take-out commitment." See also *commitment fee*.

Cooperative.   Similar to a *condominium*, but ownership of the building is generally vested in the entity with the respective owners having a right to occupy a specific unit. Operation, maintenance, and control of the building is exercised by a governing board elected by the owners.

Default.   The failure to fulfill a contractual agreement.

Deficiency judgment.   A court adjudication given when the collateral pledged for a loan in default does not satisfy the debt.

Depreciation.   As defined by generally accepted accounting principles: the systematic and rational allocation of the historical cost of depreciable assets (tangible assets, other than inventory, with limited lives of more than one year) over their useful lives.

Development costs.   Costs incurred in the creation of property and the subsequent expenditures required to bring it to an efficient status of operation, as distinguished from the costs directly expended upon the construction of the property.

Development loans.   Generally short-term first mortgage loans which finance the site development costs such as utilities, drainage, sewage systems, road systems, and recreational *amenities*. Such loans are usually repaid from the proceeds of *construction loans* or from the proceeds of the sale of segments of the developed land.

Equity kicker. An interest in the equity of a property given to a lender as a condition of obtaining a loan, most often utilized in the case of mortgages.

Escrow. Money, securities, instruments, or other property or evidences of property deposited by two or more persons, with a third person, to be delivered on a certain contingency or on the happening of a certain event.

Exculpatory clause. A provision in an agreement limiting the recourse of one party to the agreement against the other party to the agreement in the event of default. The most common example is the nonrecourse mortgage which limits recovery to the property itself. See *nonrecourse debt*.

Fair value. The amount a willing seller would expect to receive and a willing buyer would expect to pay for assets in a current sale other than in a forced or liquidation sale.

Fee simple. Unqualified ownership of real property without limitation to any particular class of heirs or restrictions.

Gap commitment. An agreement by a lender to make funds available for the difference between the unconditional minimum and maximum amount of a permanent mortgage loan commitment. Institutional lenders often issue commitments to invest in permanent first mortgage loans on income-producing properties which contain a provision fixing an unconditional minimum amount above which the lender will not fund until certain rental, occupancy, or other requirements are satisfied. The unconditional minimum amount of such a commitment is typically 80 percent to 85 percent of the face amount of the total commitment. The remaining 20 percent to 15 percent constitutes a "gap" in the commitment. In the event a lender were called upon to fund its gap commitment, the security for its mortgage loan would be subordinate to the lien of the first mortgage on the property.

General partnership. An association in which each partner has unlimited liability. Each partner usually has significant influence over the business and assumes joint and several liability for all partnership debts.

Ground lease. A lease which grants the right of use and occupancy of land.

Highest and best use. That reasonable and probable use that will support the highest present value as of the effective date of the *appraisal*. See also *market value*.

Imputed interest. An amount, as required by Accounting Principles Board Opinion No. 21, by which the stated value of a note or other instrument must be adjusted so that its carrying amount as of the date of the transaction represents the market value of the note.

Industry segment. A component of an enterprise engaged in providing a product or service or a group of related products and services primarily to unaffiliated customers for a profit.

Joint venture. Joint ventures are in many ways like general partnerships and, if unincorporated, are treated as such for tax purposes. The main distinction between a joint venture and a partnership is that usually (but not always) the joint venture is a special association for a specific enterprise or project, such as constructing a building or large-scale land development or operating an income-producing property.

Junior mortgage loans. Generally second or third mortgage loans made to finance additions to or renovations of completed structures. Junior loans are subordinate to prior mortgages.

Leverage. The use of fixed cost debt to acquire an asset in the expectation of a resulting higher rate of return on the net investment and with the correspondingly higher risk of loss.

Limited partner. A passive investor in a limited partnership who has no personal liability beyond his investment.

Limited partnership. A form of partnership having two classes of partners: (a) general partners who manage the partnership, subject to the partnership agreement, and have personal liability for the general obligations of the partnership and (b) *limited partners*.

Market value. The highest price, in terms of money, which a property will bring in a competitive and open market under all conditions requisite to a fair sale, the buyer and seller each acting prudently, knowledgeably and assuming the price is not affected by undue stimulus. See *highest and best use*.

Net realizable value. Estimated selling price in the ordinary course of business less the estimated costs to complete such property to the condition used in determining the estimated selling price and the estimated costs to dispose of the property. In some cases, the definition would also include a reduction for the estimated costs to hold the property to the estimated point of sale, including future interest and property taxes.

Nonrecourse debt.   Debt agreements secured by real estate containing *exculpatory clauses* providing that the lender has no claim against the debtor in the event of default but can only recover the property.

OILSR.   Office of Insterstate Land Sales Registration, a unit of HUD responsible for registration of interstate retail land sales programs.

Offsite costs.   Costs incurred, other than actual construction costs of the buildings, for the improvement and development of the project (sometimes referred to as *common costs*); includes such items as streets, parks, and sewer mains.

Onsite costs.   Costs incurred for the actual construction of the buildings.

Option.   A legal contract which permits, but does not require, one to buy, sell or lease real property for a stipulated period of time in accordance with specified terms. A unilateral right to exercise a privilege.

Percentage of completion method.   A method of revenue recognition used in connection with long-term construction contracts when it is possible to estimate reasonably the percentage of completion and the ultimate sales price and total costs.

Points.   Amounts paid by the borrower, generally as an adjustment to stated interest, to reflect the actual cost of borrowing money, although in certain circumstances they may be considered as service fees.

Prepayment penalty.   An extra charge for the payment of a mortgage or other debt instrument prior to its due date. Such charge is provided for in the debt instrument and is normally expressed as a percentage of the loan or an additional interest charge.

Recourse debt.   Debt agreement secured by real property which provides the lender with legal rights against the debtor beyond the property value; the equivalent of a general obligation of the debtor. See *nonrecourse debt.*

Release clause.   A provision in an agreement that, upon payment of a specified sum to the mortgage holder, the lien as to a specified portion of property will be removed from the blanket lien on the mortgaged property.

Rent-up period.   That interval of time during which a rental property is in the process of initial leasing until normal occupancy is achieved. The interval generally begins upon completion of construction.

Retail land developer. An entity or individual engaged in the development of land for volume sales to individuals on a lot basis.

Sinking fund depreciation method. A method of depreciation comprised of two elements: a fixed amount derived from interest tables, and a hypothetical interest amount calculated on the accumulated depreciation balance.

Standby commitment. An agreement by a lender to make funds available at any time within a specified period of time. The purpose of this type of commitment is to assure the potential borrower of intermediate or permanent financing if he is unable to obtain such financing on more favorable terms, thereby enabling the borrower to obtain short-term construction financing.

Subordination. A contractual arrangement, whereby a party having a claim to certain assets agrees to make his claim junior or subordinate to the claims of another party.

Syndication. A grouping of persons or legal entities who combine to carry through some financial transaction or who undertake some common venture. A syndication can take many different legal forms, such as a *limited partnership, general partnership* or *joint venture.*

Tax shelter. An investment which offers temporary deferral of income taxes or opportunities to claim allowable deductions from taxable income.

Wrap-around mortgage. A mortgage subordinate to but inclusive of an existing mortgage(s) on a property. In general, a third party lender refinances the property by extending to the borrower an amount equal to the difference between the face amount on the new mortgage and the balance outstanding on the existing mortgage(s). This difference is, in effect, a *junior mortgage.* See also *all-inclusive trust deed.*

Yield. Money paid or earned as a return on capital or investment.

Zoning. Public regulation of the permitted uses of real estate in specific areas.

Selected Reference Sources

American Institute of Certified Public Accountants. *Accounting Guide: Accounting for Profit Recognition on Sales of Real Estate.* New York: 1973, 38 p.

American Institute of Certified Public Accountants. *Accounting Guide: Accounting for Retail Land Sales.* New York: 1973, 41 p.

American Institute of Certified Public Accountants. *Accounting Principles Board Opinion No. 18; Interpretation 18–2,* "Equity Method of Accounting for Investments in Common Stock." New York: March 1971.

American Institute of Certified Public Accountants. *Accounting Principles Board Opinion No. 21,* "Interest on Receivables and Payables." New York: August 1971.

American Institute of Certified Public Accountants. *Accounting Principles Board Opinion No. 29,* "Accounting for Nonmonetary Transactions." New York: May 1973.

American Institute of Certified Public Accountants. *Audit Guide: Audits of Construction Contractors.* New York: May 1965, 102 p.

American Institute of Certified Public Accountants. Exposure Draft of Audit and Accounting Guide: Audit and Accounting Guide for Construction Contractors. New York: December 1979

American Institute of Certified Public Accountants. Exposure Draft of Statement of Position, "Accounting for Performance of Construction-Type and Certain Production-Type Contracts." New York: December 21, 1979.

American Institute of Certified Public Accountants. *Exposure Draft of Statement of Position,* "Accounting for Real Estate Acquisition, Development, and Construction Costs." July 23, 1979.

American Institute of Certified Public Accountants. *Exposure Draft of Statement of Position,* "Valuation of Certain Real Estate and Loans and Receivables Collateralized by Real Estate." New York: May 25, 1976.

American Institute of Certified Public Accountants. *Statement of Position No. 75–2,* "Accounting Practices of Real Estate Investment Trusts." New York: June 27, 1975.

American Institute of Certified Public Accountants. *Statement of Position No. 75–4,* "Presentation and Disclosure of Financial Forecasts." New York: August 1975.

American Institute of Certified Public Accountants. *Statement of Position No. 75–6,* "Questions Concerning Profit Recognition on Sales of Real Estate." New York: December 1975.

American Institute of Certified Public Accountants. *Statement of Position No. 78–2,* "Accounting Practices of Real Estate Investment Trusts (an amendment of SOP 75–2)." New York: May 12, 1978.

American Institute of Certified Public Accountants. *Statement of Position No. 78–3,* "Accounting for Costs to Sell and Rent, and Initial Rental Operations of, Real Estate Projects." New York: June 30, 1978.

American Institute of Certified Public Accountants. *Statement of Position No. 78–4,* "Application of the Deposit, Installment, and Cost Recovery Methods in Accounting for Sales of Real Estate." New York: June 30, 1978.

American Institute of Certified Public Accountants. *Statement of Position No. 78–9,* "Accounting for Investments in Real Estate Ventures." New York: December 29, 1978.

American Institute of Certified Public Accountants. *Statement on Auditing Standards No. 6,* "Related Party Transactions." New York: 1975.

American Institute of Certified Public Accountants. *Statement on Auditing Standards No. 11,* "Using the Work of a Specialist." New York: December 1975.

Canadian Institute of Chartered Accountants. *Research Study No. 11,* "Accounting for Real Estate Development Operations." Toronto: 1971.

Financial Accounting Standards Board. *Statement of Financial Accounting Standard No. 13,* "Accounting for Leases." Stamford, Conn.: November 1976, 121 p.

Financial Accounting Standards Board. *Statement of Financial Accounting Standard No. 14,* "Financial Reporting for Segments of a Business Enterprise." Stamford, Conn.: December 1976, 58 p.

Financial Accounting Standards Board. *Statement of Financial Accounting Standard No. 15,* "Accounting by Debtors and Creditors for Troubled Debt Restructurings." Stamford, Conn.: June 1977, 84 p.

Financial Accounting Standards Board. *Statement of Financial Accounting Standard No. 33,* "Financial Reporting and Changing Prices." Stamford, Conn.: September 1979, 127 p.

Financial Accounting Standards Board. *Statement of Financial Accounting Standard No. 34,* "Capitalization of Interest Cost." Stamford, Conn.: October 1979, 31 p.

Klink, James J. "Accounting for Real Estate Sales—It's a New Ball Game." *Price Waterhouse Review* (2), 1973; *Real Estate Today,* February 1974; *The CPA Journal,* February 1974.

Klink, James J. and Carol A. Fuentes (nee White). "The Accountants Reshape the Retail Land Sales Industry," *Real Estate Review.* Boston: Warren, Gorham & Lamont, Spring 1973, pp. 47–53.

Price Waterhouse & Co. *Accounting for Condominium Sales.* New York: 1975, 56 p.

Price Waterhouse & Co. *Accounting for Sales of Real Estate.* New York: 1977, 65 p.

Price Waterhouse & Co. *Cost Accounting for Real Estate Developments.* New York: 1979, 26 p.

Price Waterhouse & Co. *Investor Accounting for Real Estate Ventures.* New York: 1979, 47 p.

Price Waterhouse & Co. *Surveys of Accounting and Reporting Practices of Real Estate Developers.* New York: 1978, 56 p.; 1977, 81 p.; and 1976, 74 p.

Securities and Exchange Commission. *Accounting Series Release No. 95,* "Accounting for Real Estate Transactions Where Circumstances Indicate the Profits Were Not Earned at the Time the Transactions Were Recorded." Washington, D.C.: December 28, 1962.

Securities and Exchange Commission. *Accounting Series Release No. 142,* "Reporting Cash Flow and Other Related Data." Washington, D.C.: March 15, 1973.

Securities and Exchange Commission. *Accounting Series Release No. 162,* "Requirement for Financial Statements of Certain Special Purpose Limited Partnerships." Washington, D.C.: September 27, 1974.

Securities and Exchange Commission. *Accounting Series Release No. 166,* "Disclosure of Unusual Risks and Uncertainties in Financial Reporting." Washington, D.C.: December 23, 1974.

Securities and Exchange Commission. *Guide 60,* "Preparation of Registration Statements Relating to Interests in Real Estate Limited Partnerships." Washington, D.C.: March 1976.

Securities and Exchange Commission. *Release No. 5347,* "Guidelines as to the Applicability of the Federal Securities Laws to Offers and Sales of Condominiums or Units in a Real Estate Development." Washington, D.C.: January 4, 1973.

Securities and Exchange Commission. *Release No. 5382,* "Advertising and Sales Practices in Connection with Offers and Sales of Securities Involving Condominium Units and Other Units in Real Estate Developments." Washington, D.C.: April 1973.

Securities and Exchange Commission. *Release No. 11079,* "Annual Reports to Security Holders—Distribution of Information Statements—Rules Changes Adopted." Washington, D.C.: October 31, 1974.

Securities and Exchange Commission. *Staff Accounting Bulletin, Topic 10E,* "Offsetting Assets and Liabilities." Washington, D.C.: November 4, 1975.

United States Department of Housing and Urban Development, Office of Interstate Land Sales Registration. *Federal Register,* "Condominium and Other Construction Contracts," 39 (41), February 28, 1974.

Index